Forestry Commission
Handbook 9

Growing Broadleaves for Timber

Gary Kerr
Silviculturist

Julian Evans
Chief Research Officer (South)
The Forestry Authority

LONDON : HMSO

© Crown copyright 1993
Applications for reproduction should be made to HMSO

ISBN 0 11 710314 4

FDC 2:1761·1:(410)

British Library Cataloguing in Publication Data
A CIP catalogue record for this book is available from the British Library

Keywords: Broadleaves, Establishment, Forestry, Hardwood, Timber

HMSO publications are available from:

HMSO Publications Centre
(Mail, fax and telephone orders only)
PO Box 276, London, SW8 5DT
Telephone orders 071-873 9090
General enquiries 071-873 0011
(queuing system in operation for both numbers)
Fax orders 071-873 8200

HMSO Bookshops
49 High Holborn, London, WC1V 6HB
071-873 0011 Fax 071-873 8200 (counter service only)
258 Broad Street, Birmingham, B1 2HE
021-643 3740 Fax 021-643 6510
Southey House, 33 Wine Street, Bristol, BS1 2BQ
0272 264306 Fax 0272 294515
9-21 Princess Street, Manchester, M60 8AS
061-834 7201 Fax 061-833 0634
16 Arthur Street, Belfast, BT1 4GD
0232 238451 Fax 0232 235401
71 Lothian Road, Edinburgh, EH3 9AZ
031-228 4181 Fax 031-229 2734

HMSO's Accredited Agents
(see Yellow Pages)

and through good booksellers

Acknowledgements

The authors have derived a great deal of pleasure and satisfaction preparing this Handbook for publication. However, because of the range of subjects covered it would have been an impossible task without the help of a large number of colleagues from within the Forestry Authority Research Division and outside it. We would like to record our thanks to: David Williamson, Brian Hibberd, Simon Hodge, Harry Pepper, Paul Tabbush, John Everard, Christine Cahalan, Janet Methley, Donald Thompson, John Gibbs, David Lonsdale, David Wainhouse, George Gate, Jenny Claridge, John Williams, and to Jill Shipp, June Bell, Beryl Dickinson, Hazel Payne, Sue Stiles and Pam Wright for conscientiously typing the drafts. Particular thanks are due to Graham Darrah who kindly read and commented on the whole text.

Editor's note

The Forestry Authority Research Division offers a Research Advisory Service to woodland owners. Forestry Authority researchers are able to provide expert advice within their specialist field. The Service comprises:

- advice
- consultancy
- contracts
- information services
- publications
- specialist services

Enquiries should be directed to:

The Forestry Authority	The Forestry Authority
Forest Research Station	Northern Research Station
Alice Holt Lodge	Roslin
Wrecclesham	Midlothian EH25 9SY
Farnham	Tel: 031 445 2176
Surrey GU10 4LH	Fax: 031 445 5124
Tel: 0420 23000	
Fax: 0420 23653	

Front cover

A fine oak stem being measured for diameter at breast height. *(40504)*

Back cover

Top   Felling mature oak. *(40226)*
Middle   The 'figure of oak'. *(40080)*
Bottom   Bluebells under beech, Wendover Wood, Chilterns, Buckinghamshire. *(E 8660)*

Contents

Foreword

Many broadleaved woodlands are planted and managed for purposes other than the production of timber. This does not mean that timber production with the income it brings should be neglected as an objective of management since it is usually completely compatible with other non-market objectives.

Growing broadleaves for timber is a distillation of the most up-to-date information about broadleaved silviculture in the widest sense and will be invaluable not only for those who plant primarily for timber production but also for those with a much wider range of objectives.

With its detailed technical knowledge and clear design this book is likely to appeal to a wide range of growers, ranging from farmers through management companies to large estate owners. I am sure it will play a key role in giving good advice on how best to grow and protect broadleaved trees.

R T Bradley
Head of the Forestry Authority

February 1993

Preface

The passage of nine years has confirmed the judgement of George Holmes in the Foreword to *Silviculture of broadleaved woodland* (Forestry Commission Bulletin 62) that 'it was his belief that the book would become the standard reference for broadleaved silviculture in Britain'. The aim of this Handbook is not to replace Bulletin 62 but to complement it and focus on the silvicultural principles and practices required to achieve one stated objective: growing quality broadleaved timber.

There is growing pressure on Britain's established broadleaved woodland resource and at the same time there are exciting opportunities to create new broadleaved woodlands on agricultural land and on the urban fringe. Much has been written on achieving a wide range of objectives, such as landscape, wildlife conservation, recreation and sport, in both the established and new broadleaved woodlands. However, these objectives need not be achieved at the expense of growing quality timber; indeed often many of these objectives can be effectively integrated. It is important that foresters and the new growers of broadleaved timber, in response to the increasing demands of multi-objectivity, do not lose sight of the basic principles of growing quality timber. The fact that 1100 stems per hectare has now become the norm for planting broadleaves is, perhaps, the most outward sign of such uncertainty! This Handbook examines and reasserts the principles needed to grow quality timber and underlines that on most sites this need not preclude the pursuit of other legitimate objectives.

Gary Kerr and Julian Evans

Growing Broadleaves for Timber

Summary

This Handbook describes the silvicultural principles and practices involved in growing quality hardwood timber in Britain. There are five main principles to observe:

1. Making the correct choice of species dependent on site conditions.
2. Achieving a minimum initial stocking density.
3. Ensuring effective weed control in at least the first 3 years of establishment.
4. Protecting the trees from mammal damage during the establishment period, and using efficient and effective methods to control grey squirrels at vulnerable times.
5. Recognising that different species need to be thinned according to their silvicultural characteristics and that thinning primarily aims to improve stand quality.

LA CULTURE DES ESSENCES FEUILLUES POUR BOIS D'OEUVRE
Résumé

Ce Manuel décrit les principes et les pratiques de sylviculture pour la production du bois d'oeuvre de qualité des essences feuillues au Royaume-Uni. Il faut observer cinq principes importants:

1. Faire le choix correct des essences selon les conditions des sites.

2. Obtenir un minimum pour la densité initiale du peuplement.

3. Utiliser un désherbage efficace au moins pendant les trois années premières de l'établissement.

4. Protéger les arbres contre les dégâts par les mammifères pendant la période de l'établissement, en utilisant des méthodes efficaces et effectives de combat contre l'écureuil gris (*Sciurus carolinensis*) à des temps sensibles.

5. Reconnaître qu'il faut éclaircir les essences différentes selon leurs caractéristiques sylvicoles.

LA CULTIVACIÓN DE ESPECIES FRONDOSAS PARA MADERA
Resumo

Este Manual describe los principios y las prácticas silviculturales para la producción de madera de calidad de especies frondosas en Gran Bretaña. Debe observar cinco principios importantes:

1. Hacer la selección correcta de especies según las condiciones estacionales.

2. Obtener un mínimo de la densidad inicial de existencias.

3. Utilizar una lucha efectiva contra las malas hierbas durante al menos los tres años primeros del establecimiento.

4. Proteger los árboles contra daños por mamíferos durante el período del establecimiento, y utilizar métodos eficaces y efectivos de lucha contra la ardilla gris (*Sciurus carolinensis*) en tiempos vulnerables.

5. Reconocer que debe aclarar las especies diferentes según sus característicos silviculturales.

DER ANBAU VON LAUBBÄUMEN FÜR NUTZHOLZ
Zusammenfassung

Dieses Handbuch beschreibt die forstwirtschaftlichen Prinzipien und Verfahren, die im Anbau von Qualitätshartholz in Britannien verwendet werden. Es sind 5 Hauptprinzipien zu beachten:

1. Die richtige Wahl der, den Standortbedingungen entsprechenden, Art.

2. Das Erreichen der empfohlenen anfänglichen Mindestbestandsdichte.

3. Der Gebrauch von effektiver Unkrautkontrolle für mindestens die ersten 3 Jahre der Etablierung.

4. Der Schutz der Bäume gegen Säugetierschäden während der Etablierungsperiode, und der Gebrauch wirksamer Methoden der Grauhörnchenkontrolle in anfälligen Zeiten.

5. Das Erkennen, das verschiedene Arten entsprechend ihrer forstwirtschaftlichen Charakteristiken ausgeforstet werden müssen.

Plate 1 Britain was scoured for oak beams of a suitable specification for the restoration of the southern transept of York Minster.

(39650)

1 Growing broadleaves for timber

INTRODUCTION

- The aim of this Handbook is to describe silvicultural practices that will produce good quality hardwood timber.

- Present government policy is to encourage the management of the existing broadleaved resource (36% of woodland in Great Britain) and the establishment of new broadleaved woodland.

- It is widely acknowledged that in general the quality of British broadleaved stands is only moderate, and there is insufficient supply of high quality timber to satisfy home demand.

- Other sources of quality broadleaved timber such as the tropical forests and the temperate forests of North America cannot be guaranteed to supply our demands in perpetuity.

- At a time of increased interest in broadleaves, silvicultural practices should be directed at the production of quality hardwood.

Aim of the handbook

The purpose of this Handbook is to describe silvicultural practices that will produce high quality timber. It is recognised that other objectives such as landscaping, conservation and recreation are equally valid in managing broadleaves and can often be effectively integrated with timber production.

Policy to encourage broadleaved woodlands

In the past decade there has been a growing awareness of the importance of broadleaved woodlands. These woodlands are an integral part of the British landscape and provide a rich variety of wildlife habitats and many recreational opportunities. In addition to these benefits they produce timber which can be used in a wide range of applications.

In 1980 the Sub-Committee of the House of Lords Select Committee 'Scientific Aspects of Forestry' recommended that the continuing loss of this resource should be halted and management should be flexible enough to allow a variety of objectives. At a subsequent conference entitled 'Broadleaves in Britain' the Forestry Commission agreed to review policy on broadleaved woodland. This was carried out in consultation with over 50 other organisations representing widely different interests in woodland management. As a direct result a new policy on broadleaved woodland was published in 1985 and a new grant aid scheme was announced that was designed to encourage the management of the

Plate 2 Britain can grow quality hardwoods: good quality beech being sawn.   (39642)

existing resource and the establishment of new broadleaved woodland. More recently, additional financial incentives have been introduced that are designed to encourage the planting of trees on agricultural land in an effort to reduce agricultural surpluses in the European Community (EC).

The need for advice

In parallel with increased areas of broadleaved woodland being planted, there has been growth in the demand for advice on silvicultural practices that will result in the production of quality timber. Information is needed to satisfy, firstly, the private growers who own the vast majority of the woodlands

and, secondly, the 'new' growers: farmers, community foresters, foresters reared solely on plantation conifers and owners who are realising the potential value of their low grade woodland. A practical Handbook of this nature has been unavailable; Forestry Commission Bulletin 62 *Silviculture of broadleaved woodland* is a broad based reference work and Handbook 8 *Establishing farm woodlands* describes the establishment of woodlands on ex-agricultural land.

The broadleaved woodland resource

Extent and composition

Data for Britain's broadleaved woodland resource are given in the 1979–82 Census of Woodlands. Since then the Great Storm of October 1987 and the January storm of 1990 have occurred in which it has been estimated that a total volume of 3.1 million m³ of broadleaved trees were blown down, representing 3 % of the total British resource. The results of the Census are shown in Figures 1.1, 1.2 and 1.3. The main points illustrated are:

- Thirty-six per cent of woodland in Great Britain is broadleaved.
- Seventy-five per cent of this is high forest, however, 20 % is low grade woodland in terms of timber production.
- The main broadleaved species are oak (sessile and pedunculate), beech, ash, sycamore and birch.

Additional features of Britain's broadleaved woodlands:

- In 1980 there was an estimated 15 million m³ of wood in overmature woodland.
- Ninety per cent of the resource is privately owned.
- The area breakdown by country is 73 % in England, 18 % in Scotland and 9 % in Wales.

Table 1.1 Forecast of potential annual production of merchantable broadleaved timber from woodland and non-woodland trees, Great Britain

	Period (decade beginning)									
	1981	1991	2001	2011	2021	2031	2041	2051	2061	2071
Trees ≥ 16 cm dbh (in million m³ overbark)										
Woodland	1.24	1.24	1.54	1.58	1.93	1.70	1.18	0.99	0.73	0.72
Non-woodland	0.45	0.45	0.45	0.45	0.45	0.45	0.44	0.39	0.33	0.33
Total	1.69	1.69	1.99	2.03	2.38	2.15	1.62	1.38	1.06	1.05

Source: Broadleaves in Britain: A consultative paper. Forestry Commission, 1984.

Non-woodland resource

Non-woodland trees comprise a significant proportion of Britain's broadleaved timber resource occurring as clumps, avenues, isolated and hedgerow trees. The estimated total standing volume is 28 million m³.

Forecast of production

On the basis of the Census figures the Forestry Commission has forecast the potential annual production of merchantable broadleaved timber over the period 1980–2080 (Table 1.1). These figures indicate that there is a considerable decline in potential production throughout the 21st century, mainly in the woodland resource. However, current rates of consumption are below that potentially available leaving a reserve of timber to be carried forward; hence, the annual cut could be sustained at current levels into the 22nd century.

Quality of the resource

Very little has been recorded about the quality of the resource in terms of tree form, stain, decay and branchiness. However, it is widely acknowledged that, with some notable exceptions, the quality of British broadleaved stands is only moderate. At present more good quality timber is cut each year than is recruited from younger trees and hence the potential for supply is diminishing.

The market

The trade in British grown hardwood timber is small: in 1987 it amounted to 2.4 million m³ compared with world production of industrial hardwood of 499 million m³. Supply to the domestic market has contracted by 20 % over the past two decades; the main cause has been the decline in demand for lower grades such as mining timber. An increasing proportion of timber is imported and within this trend there is also a decline in the ratio of logs to sawnwood; this is a direct result of policies in exporting countries of adding value before export. The increase in imports indicates that a review of future prospects for British grown hardwoods must take account of trends in the world market.

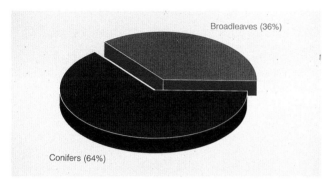

Figure 1.1 Census results: proportions of broadleaved and coniferous forest in Britain.

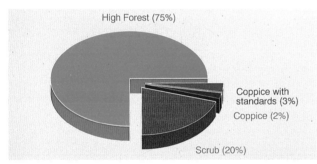

Figure 1.2 Census results: proportions of woodland types in Britain.

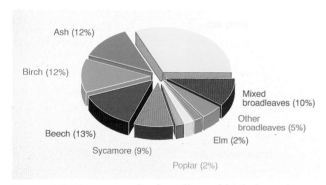

Figure 1.3 Census results: broadleaved high forest by principal species.

Plate 3 The quality of most British broadleaved stands is only moderate. (39286)

World market

World output of industrial hardwood over the period 1967–87 has increased by 52 % in response to increasing demands. The proportion of these timbers being supplied by developing countries, where the majority of the world's tropical forests are located, has been steadily growing. The Food and Agriculture Organisation in Rome in the late 1970s estimated that use of industrial hardwood was expected to increase in the period 1980–2000 by 1.8 % per annum, compared to an increase in the previous two decades of 1.5 % per annum. The difficulties in making such forecasts are demonstrated

Plate 4 Logging in Sabah, Malaysia. Unless there is a shift from exploitation to management on a sustained basis future supply of quality hardwoods from natural forests throughout the tropics may be in doubt.   (J.EVANS)

by the fact that in the interval 1982–87 consumption actually grew by 3.4 % per year. Increases of this order beg the question: where will future supplies of timber come from?

During the process of development many countries have cleared much of their natural forests. This clearance is now occurring in many developing countries and of greatest concern is the future of the world's tropical forests. As a potential supply of hardwood timber these forests represent an enormous resource. It has been estimated that they contain a growing stock of 147 billion m³ of which 10 billion m³ are currently merchantable (that is, desirable and economically accessible).

However, loss of these forests is increasingly questioned. There are many causes of deforestation, for example, conversion of land to agriculture, logging and population pressure. Wider issues such as the contribution of tropical deforestation to global warming, conservation of genepools and preservation of habitats for many rare, endangered and sometimes unknown species are also important contributary factors. Tropical deforestation is a complex issue, but we can conclude that unless there is a shift from exploitation to management on a sustained basis future supply of quality hardwoods

Plate 5 Britain spends £7 billion a year on imported timber and forest products. Quality home-grown timber could substantially reduce that figure. (E4752)

from natural forests throughout the tropics may be in doubt. Extrapolation of past supply patterns as indicators of future trends is both unwise and unrealistic.

A possible source of future supply is the temperate forests of North America which have been the source of increasing exports over the past 20 years. The United States Forest Service projection to 2030 indicates that hardwood supply is likely to exceed home demand over the same period. The onset of the European free market in 1993 and the effect of political changes in Eastern Europe are a difficult background against which to predict the availability of hardwood timber for the British market. In conclusion, although these temperate sources are possibly more stable than the tropical ones they cannot necessarily be guaranteed in the long term.

British market

This can be characterised as having two main components: a high quality and second quality market. Table 1.2 illustrates the use of British timber and imports under these two categories.

High value market

This is dominated by imports from Europe, North America and tropical countries: sources that offer consistency of quality and supply. Tropical hardwoods have penetrated the flooring and furniture markets mainly because of their decorative properties. A growing environmental awareness amongst consumers may be producing a move away from such products. North American and European imports of oak, beech and ash pose severe competition to British grown hardwoods. Quality and efficient marketing are persistent influences but their impact is governed largely by the buoyancy of different world markets and currency fluctuations.

The difference in value between high value grades and utility grades is large. Table 1.3 shows the relative values of different grades in relation to mining/pallet timber for average oak, ash and beech. Unfortunately the British resource lacks consistency of supply of high value grades and as already demonstrated the ability to sustain this in the long term is unlikely. This lack of consistency of supply does not facilitate the support of a well-developed wood processing industry. With a few important exceptions, sawmills are small and under-capitalised.

Second quality timber

Mining timber has been an important market for lower grade sawnwood produced from second class sawlogs, which account for the largest proportion of output from broadleaved woodlands. The demand for mining timber has declined since the Second World War and its future is highly dependent on British Coal policy and changes in technology. The limited number of markets for second grade sawlogs has a dramatic effect on growers' incomes since profitable processing of all grades is essential to maintain prices.

Markets for other utility uses have been stable by comparison with mining. Despite competition from softwoods hardwood pulpwood consumption is over 200 000 m³ per annum of small diameter material. Evidence from a number of sources indicates that demand for firewood will continue at 250–300 000 m³ per year.

In conclusion, there is a clear link between timber quality and market price, particularly for the best qualities. Evidence that this relationship will change in time does not exist. High prices have continued to attract quality timber from overseas; however, the future supply from these sources appears uncertain.

Table 1.2 UK markets for imported and British hardwoods in 1982

	Imported %	British %
High value		
Construction	3.3	3.8
Joinery	54.7	10.6
Furniture	30.3	9.6
Utility uses		
Transport	7.3	0.2
Others	4.4	75.8
Total	100.0	100.0

Source: Venables, R.G. (1985). The broadleaved markets. In *Growing timber for the market,* ed. P.S. Savill. Institute of Chartered Foresters, Edinburgh.

Table 1.3 Relative values of different grades in relation to mining/pallet timber for average oak, ash and beech

	Oak	Ash	Beech
Veneer	10	5.3	–
1st quality butts	6	4	2.5
Beams quality	2.5	3.3	2
Fencing quality	2	1.3	1.3
Mining/pallet timber	1	1	1

Source: Venables, R.G. (1985). The broadleaved markets. In *Growing timber for the market,* ed. P.S. Savill. Institute of Chartered Foresters, Edinburgh.

Therefore at a time of increased interest in broadleaves one major aim of silvicultural practices should be the production of good quality hardwood.

2 Choice of species

Principal broadleaves

In this Handbook it is assumed that the main objective of management is production of good quality timber from the following species.

English name	Latin name
Ash	*Fraxinus excelsior*
Beech	*Fagus sylvatica*
Cherry, wild (Gean)	*Prunus avium*
Oak, pedunculate	*Quercus robur*
Oak, sessile	*Quercus petraea*
Sweet chestnut	*Castanea sativa*
Sycamore	*Acer pseudoplatanus*

This chapter makes no mention of a large number of minor species that also produce timber; these include: alders, birches, limes, maples, willows, poplars and various exotics. Silvicultural notes on these species will be found in *Silviculture of broadleaved woodland* (Evans, 1984).

Species choice

Suitable choice of species is fundamental to the growing of quality broadleaves and is possible only if the characteristics of the site and the species are properly understood. If the wrong decision is made revenue will be reduced and production of good quality timber may even be an impossibility, no matter how intensive the silviculture. Two examples of species badly matched to site are beech grown on thin, calcareous soils and oak on light, stony, freely

ADVICE FOR SUCCESS

- Matching species with site is the foundation of good silviculture; if a poor decision is made production of quality timber may not be possible.

- In general, just six species are the main producers of quality timber: ash, beech, cherry, oak, sycamore and sweet chestnut.

- The deleterious effects of exposure on stem form usually limit the growing of quality hardwoods to areas below 300 m above sea level.

- Soil pH is one of the most important site factors to consider. Species choice is restricted on thin alkaline soils to sycamore (Italian alder and Norway maple are also well suited), but on deeper alkaline soils the choice widens to include ash, cherry and beech.

- Oak should be established on deep, fertile, acidic clays and loams because these sites are optimum for the species and are believed to reduce the incidence of shake.

- Acid, predominantly sandy, soils are generally unsuitable for growing quality hardwoods, except sweet chestnut in the south of Britain.

- A decision to grow quality hardwood must be linked to a commitment to control grey squirrels using the most effective measures (see Chapter 5).

draining soils. Beech is often associated with such sites, e.g. chalk downland, but in reality performs only moderately well on them, being frequently chlorotic, prone to beech bark disease and producing timber often of low quality. Oak growing on light, freely draining and typically stony or gravelly soils commonly produces timber which is shaken and cannot be used in any high quality application (see page 16).

A decision to use natural regeneration implies that the grower is satisfied with the suitability of the species already on the site and its genetic constitution. Planting gives greater flexibility allowing a change of species or provenance.

Choice of species may be considered under two headings:

- site conditions, mainly climate and soil;
- biological constraints.

Site conditions

Matching species to site is an integral part of good silviculture. The importance of knowledge of the previous crop and local information about the site should not be underestimated.

Options for site modifications are limited to cultivation, drainage and fertilisation. Cultivation can be achieved by ploughing, ripping, scarifying or mounding with the objective of improving the microsite around the young tree to increase survival and promote early growth. The benefits to plant growth result from improved soil aeration, more favourable soil temperature regimes and reduced weed competition. Cultivation should be considered on compacted soils, soils with thick humus layers and others with poor soil physical conditions. Drainage should be considered on waterlogged soils and in anticipation of re-wetting (see page 24). Whenever a site has been modified there is an addi-

Plate 6 Oak should be established on deep, fertile, acidic clays and loams; prime butt logs such as this one are unlikely to be produced on sub-optimal sites. (J.WHITE)

Table 2.1 Susceptibility to frost of principal broad-leaved species in Great Britain

Very susceptible	Ash
	Sweet chestnut
	Oak
	Beech
Moderately susceptible	Sycamore
	Cherry

tional requirement to define the best planting position (see page 26). It should be emphasised that the use of treeshelters, despite the improved microclimate, will not compensate for poor species choice.

Climate

Variations in total rainfall and mean temperature over Britain have remarkably little influence on species choice for broadleaves, though sweet chestnut does appear to require high levels of sunshine and high temperatures for good growth. Planting of sweet chestnut should therefore be mainly in the south and south-east of the country. The exposure of sites located 300 m or more above sea level can have a deleterious effect on stem form, and this largely precludes the planting of broadleaves at these altitudes when the objective is the production of quality timber, although some notable exceptions do exist.

It is important to assess elements of local climate, particularly the incidence of frost and drought. In addition aspect should be considered; usually most broadleaves will grow best on damper north and east facing slopes. Unseasonal frosts in autumn or spring are the greatest danger and can kill shoots and foliage or cause frost lift of young plants on heavy soils. Very susceptible species such as oak and ash can have newly opened foliage killed at temperatures as high as −1°C. New shoots will usually emerge to replace those killed by frost, but this often produces forking in the main stem; this is particularly undesirable if, as is likely, it occurs when trees are less than 5 metres high. The best way to minimise such problems is to avoid planting susceptible species in frost hollows; Table 2.1 shows the frost sensitivities of the principal broadleaved species grown in Britain.

After planting, the root system of a tree takes time to establish in its new environment: coarse rooted species such as oak and beech take longer than finer rooted species such as cherry and sycamore. Development can be slowed in periods of hot weather in late spring or summer when soil moisture deficits occur. Chances of survival in this period are considerably increased by careful plant handling and planting before the period of active growth.

Table 2.2 summarises the main site requirements for the principal broadleaved species.

Soil

A simple subdivision of soils into those derived from chalk and limestone (or have been heavily limed), clays and sands can be used as an initial guide to species choice. Lime-tolerant species should be selected for chalk and limestone soils. Heavy soils derived from clays can support a wide range of species, though oak is often the best choice. Acid, predominantly sandy, soils are generally unsuitable for growing quality broadleaves with the exception of sweet chestnut; use of conifers should be considered on such sites.

The main soil factors to consider when selecting broadleaved species for a particular site are soil water regime, fertility, rootable depth and soil pH.

Table 2.2 Summary of main site requirements for broadleaved species

Species	Optimum conditions	Unsuitable conditions	General remarks
Ash	An exacting species requiring good soil conditions. Grows well on fertile, deep calcareous loams, moist but well drained. Thrives on chalk and limestone where soil is deep and adequate moisture exists. Often the best trees are found in mixed woodland, particularly with oak, beech or sycamore. Plant indicators: dog's mercury, nettles, wild garlic	Avoid dry or shallow soils, grassland, heath or moorland, ill-drained ground, heavy clays. Frost hollows and exposed situations are also unsuitable. Avoid soils of pH < 4.5	Generally not suitable for large-scale planting or for use on exposed ground. Only plant ash if there is local evidence that first-class timber can be produced. It is rare to find suitable conditions except in small patches, but opportunity should be taken to use ash on these sites. Benefits from shelter and good weed control in youth
Beech	Good loams of all types if deep and well drained	Avoid frost hollows, heavy soils on badly drained sites, leached, very shallow soils and strongly calcareous ones	Beech is commonly associated with chalk and limestone areas but though moderately tolerant of calcareous soils it is not often at its best on them. It often grows well on acid soils. Benefits from a nurse on exposed areas, e.g. Scots pine. Useful for underplanting
Cherry, wild (Gean)	Deep moist soils, and also on deep loams over chalk	All infertile strongly acid soils, compacted soils and heavy clays. Exposed sites should be avoided; shallow and poorly drained soils give poor growth	One of the few trees to produce good timber and showy blossoms. Useful addition to any beech or oak woodland. Reasonably lime tolerant. Unsuitable for pure block plantings because of suscept-ibility to cherry canker and honey fungus
Oak, pedunculate and sessile	Well-aerated deep fertile loams. Grows well on fertile heavy soils and marls. (See Table 2.3 for soil differences between pedunculate and sessile)	Light, very freely drained stony soils may lead to shake. Avoid shallow, ill-drained or very infertile soils and exposed areas	Sessile oak tolerates less base rich soils than does pedunculate oak. Both species are relatively wind-firm
Sweet chestnut	Needs a deep, moderately fertile, acid soil. Best in warm, sunny localities of southern England. Optimum soil pH is 4.0–4.5	Unsuitable for the less fertile soils, frosty or exposed sites, badly drained ground or heavy clays.	When grown for timber it should not be left to reach very large size because of risk of shake
Sycamore	Well-drained fertile loams and sites rich in nitrogen and phosphorus. Tolerates wide range of soils and sites in Britain	As for ash but stands exposure	Fairly frost hardy. Stands exposure and pollution well. A useful tree as a wind-firm mixture for conifers in shelterbelts. Attractive to grey squirrels. Regenerates naturally very freely; may be invasive

Plate 7 A late spring frost has killed this young beech tree. (7920)

The most important distinction is between calcareous and non-calcareous soils; this can be tested by adding a few drops of dilute hydrochloric acid to a small sample of soil; when free calcium carbonate is present a reaction will proceed with effervescence, releasing carbon dioxide gas. Figure 2.1 summarises how these factors should be used to determine which species can be grown on different lowland soils.

Biological constraints

Grey squirrels can frequently cause severe damage to pole stage (10 to 40-year-old) crops of beech, sycamore and oak, and occasionally even other species in the period May to early August, although they do not attack cherry. Effective measures for their control are available, but they must be applied at the correct time (see Chapter 5). If proper control cannot be guaranteed then planting beech, sycamore and other susceptible species such as Norway maple is questionable.

Plate 8 A young ash tree suffering from drought. (39656)

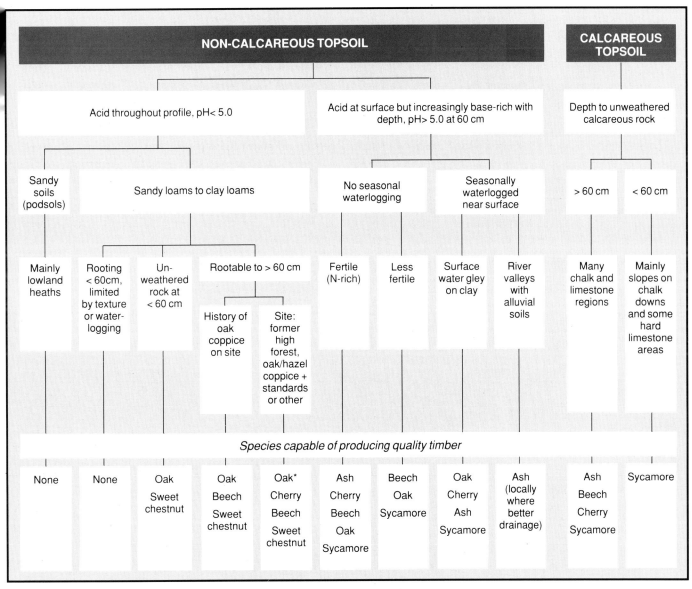

*Not on sandy loam.

Figure 2.1 Soil factors influencing choice of broadleaved species in lowland Britain.

Table 2.3 Soil requirements for oak		
	Pedunculate	**Sessile**
Nutritional status	High fertility	Moderate–high fertility
Texture	Most textures suitable, but possibly better than sessile on heavy soils, i.e. clay loams, clays	Most textures suitable, but grows better than pedunculate on lighter soils
Acidity (pH)	4.5 – 7.5	4.0 – 6.5
Drainage	More tolerant of waterlogged conditions than sessile oak	Well-drained soils
Rooting depth	Deep rooting species, at least 60 cm rootable depth, preferably > 1 m	As for pedunculate
Flooding	Mature trees tolerant, including sea water	Less tolerant of flooding than pedunculate oak

Wood properties

The main wood properties of the principal broadleaved species are summarised in Table 2.4. This should be used with reference to the following notes.

Density

Values quoted are at 15 % moisture content.

Durability

Durability is expressed as the average life of a 5 cm x 5 cm section of heartwood in ground contact.

Classification	Life in ground contact (years)
Durable	15–25
Moderate	10–15
Non-durable	5–10
Perishable	< 5

Permeability refers to the ease with which timbers can be penetrated with preservatives in standard conditions (heartwood and sapwood usually differ in permeability).

Permeability

Permeable	(1)	Easily absorbed
Moderately resistant	(2)	6–18 mm penetration in 2–3 hours
Resistant	(3)	Difficult to penetrate more than 3–6 mm
Extremely resistant	(4)	Absorbs only a small amount

Working qualities

This refers to ease of working; a 'difficult' classification does not mean that a timber is unworkable but indicates that care should be taken in machining.

Uses and supply

Information given under these headings is not exhaustive. Regional and local variation in supply and demand can be considerable.

Table 2.4 Wood property factors of broadleaved species

Species	Colour	Density kg m⁻³	Durability and permeability (1–4)	Working qualities	Serious defects	Uses	Supply
Ash	White to light brown	710	Perishable (2)	Good	Blackheart	Veneers Sports equipment Tool handles Agricultural implements Furniture	Regular but demand exceeds supply for good quality ash
Beech	White to light brown	720	Perishable (1)	Good	Pink or reddish brown colouring	Veneer Cabinet work Turnery Domestics Furniture	UK and Continental sources, but becoming scarce. UK sources generally poor quality: this may be due to poor species choice (page 8)
Cherry	Red–brown	630	Moderate (2)	Good	'Green lines' in colour	Veneer Cabinet work Furniture Domestics	Not regularly available
Oak	Heartwood yellow–brown Sapwood white	700	Heartwood durable (4) Sapwood perishable (2)	Medium/difficult	Shake	Veneer High class joinery Panelling Flooring Construction	Variable and high grades constantly in short supply
Sweet chestnut	Light yellow–brown	560	Durable (4)	Good	Shake	Veneer Construction (alternative to oak) Furniture Coffin boards Turnery	Limited
Sycamore	White or yellowish–white	630	Perishable (1)	Good	–	Veneer Furniture Turnery Textile equipment	Limited

Amended from TRADA wood information sheet No. 10 1987.

Plate 9 Chalk downland with shallow soils: a testing environment for trees. Norway maple, Italian alder or sycamore should give good response when combined with good establishment practice. (39241)

Shake

Shake is longitudinal fissuring or separation of wood found in freshly felled timber, either radiating from the pith (star shake) or as a cleavage along an annual ring (ring shake) and it can easily be confused with drying or felling cracks. Plate 10 illustrates the two types. Shake may be restricted to the lower butt or extend along the trunk and into branch wood. Presence of shake in a tree cannot be pre-dicted reliably from external signs though, when they occur, deep fissuring in the bark or longitudinal ribbing may indicate serious star shake. Shake is a serious defect greatly reducing the conversion potential of a log since the timber invariably splits or separates along the line of the shake.

Shake occurs primarily in oak and sweet chestnut. The incidence of shake within any one stand is usually very variable but the proportion of trees affected

16

Plate 10 Star shake and ring shake in oak logs.

(40248 and 38581)

appears primarily related to soil conditions. Oak on heavy soils, clays and clay loams generally has less shake than stands on lighter soils, especially stony, gravelly and sandy soils. This is borne out by the current observation that oak on heavy south-east England soils is less shaken than, for example, oak on triassic sands in the Midlands. Similarly, in the Forest of Dean most shake occurs in oak on the light, freely draining soils.

The following recommendations on where oak should be planted and silvicultural practices to minimise shake are based on Henman and Denne (1992).

Site conditions

- Good nutrient supply (calcium, magnesium and potassium levels appear to be important, particularly calcium; calcium availability of more than 1.0 mEq 100 g^{-1} is recommended).
- High clay fraction (more than 20% by Avery soil texture classification).
- Deep soil.

- Good moisture retention (may be due to higher clay and/or organic matter contents).
- Level or slightly sloping sites: avoid frost hollows.
- Avoid extreme wind exposure.

Silvicultural practices

- Avoid bark-bruising and wound damage during forest operations.
- Protect from animal damage (bark-stripping, etc.), especially in young crops.
- Protect from fire.
- If pruning, exercise care to minimise wound infection (see Chapter 6).
- Maintain an even growth rate, by planning thinning and understorey removal to minimise sudden changes in ring width.

Although no remedial treatment for shake can be applied in existing crops, research by Savill and Mather (1990) has determined a method for identifying trees prone to shake, so that they can be

Uses of broadleaved timber

Ash: *Fraxinus excelsior.*

Ash is the toughest of British grown woods and many of its uses require toughness. British ash from straight, vigorous growth trees is preferred to ash from elsewhere. Good quality ash is used in furniture and outstanding trees are used for veneer. It is a useful estate timber, though not for use in ground contact unless treated; it is accepted for pulp and makes an excellent fuelwood owing to low moisture content.

Beech: *Fagus sylvatica.*

Available at modest cost and in good supply, both from Britain and elsewhere in Europe, beech is the most commonly used hardwood in Britain. It is the foremost furniture wood, especially for chairs and tables, as it machines well, is strong and has a uniform pale appearance suitable for a variety of finishes. Wood of good quality – straight grained, clean and free from growth defects – is sought for most furniture, but lower quality is used for the framing of upholstered furniture. Beech is used for tool handles and other turned items, domestic ware, especially kitchenware, and toys, and it makes a hard-wearing domestic floor. Timber from misshapen trees can be difficult to market but it makes excellent firewood and in appropriate sizes is accepted for hardwood pulp.

Cherry: *Prunus avium.*

It is a most attractive wood available in limited supply and only modest sizes. Cherry is sought by craftsmen for cabinet making and furniture, for panelling and decorative joinery. It has an assured market and is unlikely to be in over-supply but must be well grown as timber marred by growth blemishes is difficult to market for other than low grade uses.

Oak: *Quercus robur, Q. petraea.*

Oak varies greatly in quality, depending on straightness of grain and presence of knots, epicormics, internal splits, stain, etc., with the best timber commanding a price ten times that of the poorest. Top quality logs are used for veneer and other high quality timber in furniture, joinery, panelling, flooring and ships' planking.

Large sections are used in heavy construction, boat building, canal and harbour works. Lesser quality oak is sawn for estate, farm and garden uses, for posts, fencing and where there is a need for decay resistance. Galvanised fastenings should be used as the heartwood corrodes iron in moist conditions. Roundwood is split for posts, is accepted for hardwood pulp and makes excellent firewood.

Sweet chestnut: *Castanea sativa.*

Sweet chestnut is an attractive, underrated wood obtained from coppice and larger trees, though old trees tend to have internal splits and spiral grain. With a minimal sapwood, coppice stems make excellent stakes and poles for estate work, though galvanised fastenings should be used as the heartwood corrodes iron in moist conditions. Sawnwood makes durable posts, gates, etc. and the wood is cleft for fencing. Select wood is used for exterior and interior joinery and for furniture; fine logs command a good price for veneer.

Sycamore: *Acer pseudoplatanus.*

Sycamore is an attractive, blond wood used in cabinet work and for furniture framing. The wood is also popular for kitchen items, bread and chopping boards, for dairy items, and for wooden rollers, brush handles and similar items. Small roundwood is used for pulp and burns well when dry, though it is not as dense as some other hardwoods. Outstanding logs and especially those with a wavy grain are cut for veneer and command a high price.

removed in thinnings. This is based on the finding that oak trees that flush later in spring have a greater tendency to shake.

Colour defects

The three most serious colour defects occurring in the six principal broadleaves which usually reduce their value are: brown colouring of beech, green lines or veins in cherry and blackheart in ash. All of these defects are ubiquitous but variation exists in the measures the grower can employ to minimise their incidence. There is little knowledge on the causes of brown colouring of beech or green lines in cherry. Only past experience of the site may indicate the proportion of affected trees; if high, further planting of the species is questionable. Greater knowledge exists on the causes of blackheart in ash and hence the grower has more control on its incidence. It can be reduced by avoiding the following:

- planting ash on wet, swampy ground;
- growing on long rotations of 80+ years;
- storing ash coppice.

However, not all variations in wood properties reduce value; brown oak, burr oak and curly grain in sycamore can all command a price premium.

Tree improvement

Tree improvement is a combination of tree breeding (the production of genetically superior stock) and silviculture to improve the economic return from a crop. The main objectives of work on broadleaved trees are:

- To improve form: cylindrical straight stems, absence of low forking, absence of epicormics and light branching are all desirable characteristics which improve quality.

- To identify provenances and varieties better suited to particular site conditions; little is known about this subject for broadleaves. This situation is being rectified by the establishment of provenance trials. The use of local seed origins appears reasonably safe and where possible beech should be from Kingscote, Gloucestershire or Forêt de Soignes, Brabant Region, south of Brussels, Belgium.

- To improve wood quality: spiral grain is a problem in some species (e.g. sweet chestnut) and shake is also a problem in oak and sweet chestnut; reducing these will improve quality.

- To improve disease resistance.

References

Evans, J. (1984). *Silviculture of broadleaved woodland.* Forestry Commission Bulletin 62. HMSO, London.

Henman, G.S. and Denne, M.P. (1992). *Shake in oak.* Forestry Commission RIN 218. The Forestry Authority.

Savill, P.S. and Mather, R.A. (1990). A possible indicator of shake in oak: relationship between flushing dates and vessel sizes. *Forestry* **63**, 355–362.

Plates 11–16 The 'figure' of the six principal broadleaved species.

Plate 11 Ash: *Fraxinus excelsior.* Ash typically produces a white wood, though on wet or other unfavourable growth sites it can develop a core of dark wood, which is disliked by users. Growth rings are conspicuous giving clean white wood a particularly attractive figure. The wood is heavy, comparable to beech, although the weight varies depending on vigour of growth. It is an easy wood to handle as it dries readily and can be sawn and machined to a good finish; once dry it is fairly stable in use. Although ash is stronger than oak, it is not as durable in conditions favouring decay unless treated with preservative. (40079)

Plate 12 Beech: *Fagus sylvatica.* Beech is white when first cut but becomes a very pale brown on drying and exposure. Well grown, it is straight grained, with a fine texture and a characteristic ray figure which, if much less obvious than that in oak, is seen on both flat sawn and radial surfaces. Beech is a heavy wood, comparable in weight to a tough oak, and is one of the strongest British timbers. It is not durable where there is a risk of decay but it is readily treated with preservatives. (40077)

Plate 13 Cherry: *Prunus avium.* Cherry has a pinkish-brown heartwood with a well-defined paler sapwood, typically straight grained and with a fine, even texture. Cherry is lighter in weight than beech and not quite as strong. It is moderately durable in conditions favouring decay but, generally, should not be considered for outdoor use. (40074)

20

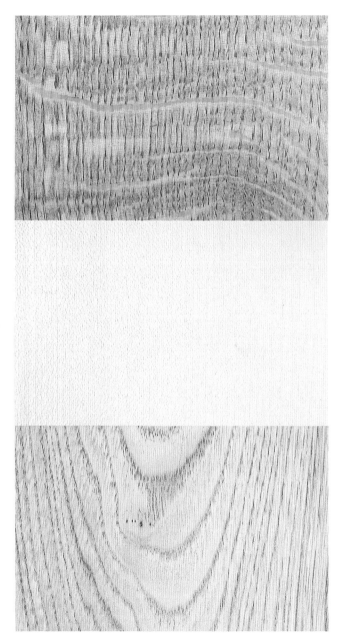

Plate 14 Oak: *Quercus robur, Q. petraea.* The best-known British wood, oak is pale brown, coarse-textured, typically straight grained and with a conspicuous silver-grain figure when quarter sawn; it has a well-defined, pale sapwood. Oak is more variable in character than most woods, with British timber typically heavy, strong and tough from vigorous growth trees; that from old or slowly grown trees is softer and milder. The two species have similar woods which are not distinguished commercially. The heartwood has excellent decay resistance but sapwood is perishable, is liable to insect attack and must be excluded or given preservative treatment if long-term service is required. (40080)

Plate 15 Sycamore: *Acer pseudoplatanus.* Sycamore has an almost white wood with a distinctive growth ring figure on flat sawn surfaces and a high natural lustre, especially on quarter sawn stock. The texture is fine and even and the grain generally straight, but occasionally wavy giving a characteristic fiddle-back figure. Sycamore is somewhat lighter in weight than beech and not as strong. Sycamore dries rapidly and well but care is needed in kiln drying to retain a white colour and protracted air drying can result in staining; once dry, it is fairly stable in use and works well to give an excellent finish. It is quickly damaged by fungi in conditions favouring decay but it is easily treated with preservatives. (40076)

Plate 16 Sweet chestnut: *Castanea sativa.* Sweet chestnut produces an attractive, warm yellow-brown wood resembling a plain oak in colour and texture but lacking the silver grain figure of oak; there is a very narrow, pale sapwood ring, much less than in oak. The grain is straight in young stems but tends to spiral as the tree ages. Sweet chestnut is of medium weight, some 20 % lighter than oak and correspondingly lower in strength. It dries slowly and care is needed to avoid degrade; once dry, it is one of the most stable British woods. It is easier to saw and machine than oak and, like oak, the heartwood has an excellent resistance to decay. (40078)

21

3 Establishment and maintenance

- To grow quality broadleaves it is essential to achieve an adequate initial stocking of main crop species. Recommendations vary with species and on new planting or restocking sites (see Table 3.1).

- Early side shelter is essential.

- The use of bare-rooted plants is recommended, height 20–50 cm, root collar diameter 5.0–9.0 mm, combined with careful plant handling and planting in autumn or early spring.

- Treeshelters assist the establishment of broadleaved trees by providing an improved microclimate and considerable protection. However, they are not a panacea and should only be used after consideration of their limitations, e.g. fencing may be a more cost-effective and permanent option for large planting sites.

- Effective weed control is essential for successful tree establishment. Treeshelters are not a substitute for weeding.

- Conifer : broadleaved mixtures must be effectively managed; if neglected they may produce little, if any, quality broadleaved timber.

Plate 17 Close initial spacing in a naturally regenerated area in the Forest of Dean: this offers a high potential to produce quality timber.

(4d 04/91)

Table 3.1 Recommended minimum initial stocking for production of quality timber

Species	Stocking stems per hectare (square spacing, m)		Remarks
	New planting	*Restocking*[a]	
Ash	2500 (2.0)	1600 (2.5)	Standard recommendation for growing quality broadleaves
Sweet chestnut	2500 (2.0)	1600 (2.5)	As for ash
Sycamore	2500 (2.0)	1600 (2.5)	As for ash
Beech	3100 (1.8)	2500 (2.0)	Considerable variation between individuals: selection of final crop must take place from a high initial stocking
Oak	3100 (1.8)	2500 (2.0)	Weak apical dominance: as for beech
Cherry	1100 (3.0)	1100 (3.0)	Strong apical dominance. Pruning will be essential to prevent heavy low branching

[a] Not including woody infill.

This chapter primarily concerns restocking clear-felled and group felled woodland and planting of new ground. Many of the silvicultural principles also apply when planting is used to supplement natural regeneration: this is considered specifically in the next chapter.

Stocking

To grow quality broadleaves it is essential to secure an adequate initial stocking by planting or natural regeneration. The figure of 1100 stems per hectare (3.0 m square spacing) has become synonymous with the planting of broadleaves because it is the *minimum* stocking allowable for full Forestry Authority grant aid. It must be recognised that the establishment of 1100 stems per hectare will not assure production of quality timber. Table 3.1 gives recommendations for the minimum initial stocking of the principal broadleaves. This differentiates between restocking and new planting sites, recommended stocking on the former being lower because supplementary natural regeneration and coppice from such species as ash, sycamore, willow and birch will often occur. Such woody growth provides valuable side shelter.

Preparation for planting

The aim of site preparation is to secure establishment and rapid early growth. Four problems are likely to occur:

- restricted access to the planting position;
- re-wetting of soil on restocking sites;
- competition from dense weed growth;
- damage caused by browsing animals.

Access to planting position

Lop and top can hinder planting and access for subsequent maintenance; it can also harbour damaging mammals. The problem should be dealt with during the harvesting operation. If a market for lop and top can be found then it should be sold and removed from site. However, if no market exists, the contract should specify treatment of lop and top which must be strictly imposed, e.g. burning, chopping or leaving trimmed and evenly spread.

Re-wetting

When trees are felled, more water reaches the ground, and less is removed by transpiration. As a result, the water table can rise and can cause waterlogging or re-wetting. This is particularly serious on clay soils, making the site inhospitable to new plants and working conditions difficult. In addition to the vegetational changes caused by felling, species indicating surface water, e.g. tussock grass and rushes, invade the site. The presence of extra water also renders the site more frost prone. Excess water restricts the supply of oxygen to roots and is a frequent cause of plant failure. If experience on similar sites suggests very serious re-wetting, drainage should be considered prior to planting or an overstorey (20 %) of the former crop retained for 5–10 years after replanting. An additional option if employing group regeneration is to use small coupe sizes.

Weed control

This essential operation is considered in more detail later in the chapter.

Protection

Protection of newly planted trees against mammals is usually necessary, and should be considered during site preparation. More detail is given in Chapter 5.

Planting stock

When purchasing planting stock every effort should be made to inspect the plants in the nursery. When they are received plants must be healthy, well balanced (at least an even root:shoot ratio), undamaged and free from pests and diseases.

Plant type

Research evidence indicates that there are no clear and consistent survival and growth benefits from the use of cell-grown stock, although, perhaps, they are less prone to poor handling than bare-rooted stock. Hence factors such as scale and remoteness of planting, expertise of those undertaking the planting, requirement to fit planting around other work programmes and relative prices of bare-root and cell-grown stock should be the main determinants of which stock type is used.

Size of plant

Table 3.2 is a guide to the optimum size ranges for bare-rooted planting stock. Although height is the most common method of size grading, root collar diameter is the more important of the two criteria. The size range is usually produced after 1 or 2 years in the nursery, either 1+1 transplants or 1u1 or $\frac{1}{2}u\frac{1}{2}$

Plate 18 It is essential to plant good quality trees; inspection in the nursery is recommended. (40215)

Plate 19 Most bare-root transplants for forestry use are between 20 and 50 cm high and should have at least 5 mm root collar diameter. This stock type is cheap, easy to transport and easy to plant. (40276)

Plate 20 Cell-grown stock: in research trials survival and growth has not been consistently better than transplants, but cell-grown stock is less prone to handling damage than bare-root stock. (40274)

undercuts. Larger plants than indicated confer no lasting advantage, can stagnate for a year or two after planting and are much more expensive.

Plant handling

There are many possible reasons for the failure of planting stock but the main cause of death is often poor plant handling. Many failures can be avoided if care is taken over the handling of plants at every stage from the nursery bed to where they are finally planted. Damage occurs in three main ways.

1. Root drying: with increasing temperatures and increasing air movement roots will dry out faster. If the plants are lifted in the nursery on windy days the operation should be screened to protect the plants. After placement in specially designed storage bags, which are immediately sealed, the plants should next emerge from the bags shortly before planting. During planting the plants should be kept in a windproof planting bag and lifted out individually.

2. Overheating: bright sunshine on a plant, box or vehicle can create very high temperatures. Plants (in bags) should always be kept cool and out of direct sunlight.

3. Physical damage: broken shoots or roots can be seen, but physical damage which is not visible to the naked eye is just as important. Plants should always be treated with great care and never thrown around. When planting, the ball of the foot (not a spade or heel of the foot) should be used to firm roots gently into the ground.

Planting

Notch planting is a suitable method for all broadleaved species. A spade is used to cut a T- or L-shaped slit in the ground; after making the second cut the spade is used to lever open the first slit and the root system is gently placed into the notch ensuring even root distribution and no bends or breaks. Also, ensure the plant is left vertical and not leaning or bent to one side. Pit planting is an acceptable, if more expensive, method of planting broadleaved trees.

Planting position

Generally broadleaves should be planted into mineral soils. If a surface layer of humus exists this should be scraped away with the boot or spade. When cultivation or drainage is used the microsite for planting will be either raised or lowered compared to its pre-treatment level. On poorly drained soils the best planting position is the raised one, while on freely draining mineral soils the raised or mid-planting position is best.

Time of planting

The best time to plant broadleaves is between late October and mid-December during mild weather, providing leaf fall has occurred; this gives time for root development before flushing in spring. Early spring planting, before any sign of flushing, is often successful but if it is followed by a prolonged dry spell losses can be high. In general, all planting should be completed by late March.

Beating up

If recommended initial stocking levels (Table 3.1) have been achieved there is only a requirement to beat up if losses are greater than 20 %, the exception being with mixtures where maintenance of high stocking levels is important for the main crop species. Beating up reflects some failure in the

Table 3.2 A guide to sizes for bare-rooted transplants				
	Minimum height (cm)	Minimum root collar diameter (mm)	Maximum height (recommended) (cm)	Maximum root collar diameter (mm)
Ash	20	5.0	50	9.5
Beech	20	4.0	50	7.5
Cherry	20	5.0	50	9.5
Oak	20	5.0	50	9.5
Sycamore	30	4.5	50	6.0
Sweet chestnut	20	5.0	50	9.5

Minimum heights and stem diameters from British Standard Nursery Stock, Specification for Forest Trees (BS3936: Part 4: 1984).

regeneration phase and it is important to review each stage to identify the most likely cause so that future corrective action can be taken.

Stumping back

This is a practice of cutting back top growth, to about 10 cm above ground, a few years after planting to stimulate damaged or poorly formed trees to resprout a straight new stem. It should not be used on beech.

Treeshelters

Treeshelters are translucent plastic tubes up to 2 m tall that are placed around trees to aid establishment. They solve many problems faced during the establishment of broadleaved trees. However, they are not a panacea for the planting of broadleaves and should not be used without consideration of their limitations. Fencing may be a cheaper and permanent option for large planting sites (> 2 ha); damage by mammals can often occur after the treeshelter has degraded or been removed.

Benefits of treeshelters

- Increased plant survival during establishment.
- Enhanced early height growth for all species listed in Table 3.3.
- Trees in treeshelters are easy to locate and herbicides can be applied easily.
- Cost-effective protection from browsing animals for small scale plantings.

Treeshelter design

Once a decision to use treeshelters has been made consideration must be given to the design as several types are available on the market. The relevance of the following factors should be evaluated.

Plate 21 Careless handling of trees reduces their quality. (40270)

Plate 22 A well-established ash transplant protected by a vole guard. (39251)

Size Height must be above the maximum browse level of the damaging mammal (see Table 5.3).

Cross sectional shape Square: can be flat packed to ease storage and transport but they can blow flat in strong winds.
Round: less prone to damage by wind than square shapes; more bulky even though differing diameters nest together for storage and transport.

Stake This is usually wooden, cleft chestnut or treated softwood, size 25 mm x 25 mm, driven 30 cm into the ground. When erected it should be shorter than the treeshelter to avoid stem abrasion at the point where the tree will be above the rim of the treeshelter.

Ties These should be quick and easy to secure and release to allow inspection and maintenance.

Lip The lip of the shelter should not be sharp to avoid abrasion or even decapitation of soft leading shoots as found in ash, for example.

Colour Colour should be chosen to blend in with the local landscape, light brown and some shades of green being particularly acceptable in this respect. When light levels are low, e.g. underplanting, clear or white treeshelters should be used.

Planting design

Treeshelters should not be used in geometric patterns unless tractor access is required for maintenance. The main justification for straight rows has been the difficulty in locating young trees after planting; with treeshelters this is not a problem.

Plate 23 Treeshelters can be an effective aid to tree establishment, however, they are not a 'plant and leave' option.
(E8596)

Maintenance

Most treeshelters are manufactured from polypropylene formulated to begin to break down after 5–10 years exposure to ultraviolet light. The shelters should not be removed before this time otherwise the tree may not be sturdy enough to stay erect. As the plastic degrades it will be necessary to clear the larger pieces of debris to prevent a litter problem. Treeshelters are *not* a substitute for weeding and normal weed control practice should be followed.

Table 3.3	Effects of treeshelters on growth by species			
Species	**Overall growth response**[a]			**Comments**
	Very good	**Good**	**Initial**	
Ash		✔		
Beech	✔			Poor response in presence of beech woolly aphid (see Table 5.5)
Cherry			✔	Rapidly grows out of shelter
Oak	✔			Sometimes trees fail to respond
Sycamore		✔		
Sweet chestnut		✔		Tending to rapid initial response only

[a] Overall growth response:
1. *Very good.* Species showing consistently good response to shelters, usually more than doubling rate of height growth in first 2–3 years after planting.
2. *Good.* Generally show a significant improvement in growth on most sites but not as marked as in 1.
3. *Initial.* Species that initially respond well to shelters but, because of early emergence from the top (end of first or during second year) and naturally fast growth anyway, do not sustain a large significant improvement beyond the third year.

Table 3.4	Conifer: broadleaved compatibility				
	Norway spruce	**European larch**	**Scots pine**	**Corsican pine**	**Western red cedar**
Oak	✔	✔	✔		
Beech	✔	✔	✔	✔	✔
Ash	✔	✔			

Mixtures of species

Conifer: broadleaved mixtures

There are two main reasons for planting conifers in mixture with broadleaves:

- firstly, because of the long rotations and relatively slow growth rate of broadleaves, the conifers, which mature sooner, will produce early financial returns;
- secondly, the conifer can protect broadleaved species from frosts and also offer side shelter.

When considering whether to plant a mixture the distinction between a new planting on open ground or a restocking site is important. In both situations the advantage of early returns will hold, but if this is not a factor on a restocking site the protection can be more economically gained from natural regeneration, coppice regrowth and other woody infill.

The species planted together must be compatible in terms of early growth rate and must be planted in a pattern that will ensure survival of each species until the time of first thinning. If one species dominates the other, early intervention will be required with a financial penalty because any trees removed will not be of a marketable size. Table 3.4 is a guide to compatible species. As a rule of thumb, the estimated conifer yield class should not be more than double that of the broadleaved component except for larch when it should be no more than 50 % greater.

There are two main planting patterns for growing conifer:broadleaved mixtures. These are the strip design and the group design. The strip design involves planting three rows of conifer alternating with three rows of broadleaves; three is considered the minimum number of rows to ensure a robust design but the numbers can be varied above this figure so long as the broadleaves are at final crop spacing of 10–15 m. Row mixtures can create landscape problems with 'pyjama stripes' whereas the group pattern avoids this. Groups of 9–25 broadleaves are planted at 10–15 m centres in a matrix of conifers.

Neglected conifer:broadleaved mixtures may produce very little, if any, quality broadleaved timber. The key to success is effective management. This must aim to ensure:

- Levels of stocking that are greater than for pure species and greater attention paid to beating up.

- Effective weed control, considering the differing susceptibilities to herbicides.

- A punctual cleaning and first thinning, followed by subsequent thinnings to favour the broadleaved crop (see page 67).

- Squirrel control: conifer:broadleaved mixtures provide an excellent habitat for grey squirrels and control will be essential.

Mixtures of broadleaves

The planting of mixtures of broadleaves has become more common recently, as confirmed by a survey monitoring the new policy on broadleaved woodland which indicated that a significant amount of recent planting has consisted of mixtures of broadleaved species. Compatibility between species is less of a problem than with conifer:broadleaves due to more uniform growth rates. However, species such as ash and cherry will reach marketable sizes, if thinned correctly, sooner than oak or beech. The quality of the timber produced is unlikely to be compromised by such a practice so long as the thinning requirements for each species are catered for. However, it should be remembered that any timber produced must be sold in marketable units and the use of mixtures may result in marketing problems when used on small areas.

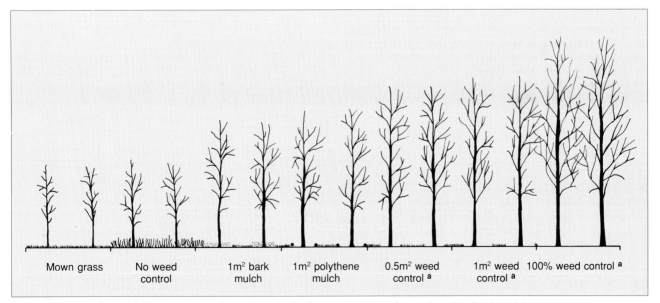

Figure 3.1 Results of different types of weed control after 3 years on cherry ([a] using herbicide).

Plate 24 Effect of weeding on cherry (4th growing season): no weeding. (40203)

Plate 25 Effect of weeding on cherry (4th growing season): 1 m² treated with herbicide. (40201)

Weed control

The need to weed

The need to weed is clearly demonstrated in plates 24 and 25. Weeds reduce the survival and early growth of newly planted trees by competing in two main ways:

- competition for soil moisture and nutrients;
- physical damage and competition for light.

Competition for soil moisture and nutrients

Only small amounts of moisture evaporate from bare soil before a layer of dry soil forms a barrier to further losses. In contrast, vegetation transpires large amounts of moisture before availability limits further loss. Cutting or mowing vegetation by perpetuating fresh regrowth can increase this rate of loss. Severe moisture stress kills trees or reduces growth and can be particularly significant in southern Britain when May and June are often warm and dry.

32

In contrast, well-weeded trees often show remarkable vigour: ash and cherry can grow 1 m in a year, and oak and beech 2.5 m in such conditions.

Moisture and nutrient competition are inter-related; weeds may compete directly for nutrients or make them unavailable by drying the soil.

Physical damage and competition for light

Tall weeds may compete for light, and they can physically damage trees when they collapse in the autumn. They also harbour bark-gnawing rodents such as voles. Mowing or cutting reduces these harmful effects, but does not reduce root competition.

Weed control methods

Herbicide application

The application of herbicides to control weeds is widely used. Where problem weeds such as bramble, bracken, gorse, rhododendron or unwanted woody regrowth are present or are anticipated to invade within one or two seasons, it may be better to control such weeds over the whole site before planting. The use of herbicides prior to planting allows a wide choice since trees do not have to tolerate direct application. The residual effects of any chemical must be considered because the trees will be planted fairly soon after the herbicide application in order to obtain maximum benefit from the weed-free conditions. The choice of which herbicide to use after planting is determined not only by the weed species to be controlled, but also by the species of trees that are present. Very few herbicides are tolerated by trees in active growth and many broadleaved tree species will not tolerate overall applications of some herbicides even during the dormant season.

Plate 26 Formative pruning of a young oak tree.   (40474)

When applying herbicide around a small tree it is difficult if not impossible to treat the weeds immediately around the base of the stem without getting any chemical on the stem or foliage of the tree. Killing these last few weeds is usually unnecessary.

For information on the choice of herbicide, method of application and safe working practice refer to Williamson and Lane (1989) and if dealing with new planting on ex-agricultural land, Williamson (1992) will be useful.

Mulching

As a method of weed control, mulching acts by smothering weeds or preventing them from germinating. It has the additional benefit of reducing or eliminating evaporation from the soil surface, keeping nutrient-rich upper soil layers moist enough to nourish tree roots. The effectiveness of mulching varies with the material used. Pine bark and bitumenized felt mulches degrade after only one growing season and thereafter provide ineffective weed control. Black polythene with an ultraviolet light inhibitor and a minimum thickness of 125 μm is a good mulch. The polythene mulching material must either be laid on bare ground or on ground where the weeds have been killed by herbicides. Black polythene mulch mats are not suitable for use on sites where tussocky grass or bracken is present because the mulching material cannot be kept in contact with the ground. Damage can occur where voles get under the mats and strip the bark off the trees. Clods of earth around the base of the tree and additionally around the outer edge of the mulch should be used to secure its position.

Figure 3.1 shows the effect of different methods of weed control on cherry after 3 years.

Area

A well-researched compromise is to keep an area of 1 m² around each tree free from weeds; this can be achieved by spot or band application of herbicide or by mulching. This area should be kept substantially free of weeds until the trees are at least 2 m tall.

Timing

Vigorous tree growth occurs in May and June and this is the time weed control is most needed. If done later in the growing season benefit will be less. Therefore optimum benefits from weed control are obtained where either residual herbicides or mulches are applied in the winter/spring in anticipation of weed competition. The application of herbicides at this time of year means that many broadleaved species are more tolerant of herbicide application. Residual herbicides also have the added advantage of being less demanding in terms of weather conditions and the date of application.

Cleaning

Cleaning is a weed control operation carried out in thicket or young pole stage stands to prevent damage to the growth and stem quality of trees by vigorous woody growth and climbers. Early and frequent removal is prudent especially if growth is slow or the regeneration phase long. (The cleaning of natural regeneration is considered on page 46.) However, complete cleaning is an expensive operation and a balance must be found between silvicultural demands and economics. Two methods of cost reduction are possible. Firstly, the removal only of climbers, thorn, sallow and other 'rank' species, leaving the other species until first thinning. Secondly, the delaying of cleaning until near the time of canopy closure; this may eliminate the need to carry out a first thinning, especially in understocked stands, though some loss of stem quality may occur.

Formative pruning

The objective of formative pruning (also called singling) is to produce a single straight stem of at least 5 m in height with small branches that will die quickly at the onset of canopy closure leaving the bole virtually defect free.

Guidelines on formative pruning are presented based on observation and some limited experimentation. Such pruning is becoming increasingly important as a remedial treatment for the poorly developing form of many timber species planted in the last 10 years on bare ground, and even some restocking sites, at wide spacings and stockings as low as 1100 stems per hectare.

Species

All species will benefit from some formative pruning but some more so than others. In general, oak and beech lack apical dominance and are most likely to require formative pruning. Ash, sweet chestnut and sycamore are more apically dominant than oak or beech and may occasionally require intervention especially if damage from frost or leader breakage is experienced. Wild cherry has strong apical dominance but at low densities will form low heavy branches which usually need removing.

When to prune and pruning position

The principles outlined in Chapter 6 in relation to pruning apply equally to formative pruning.

Branch removal

The main priority is to remove forks and hence favour the best (straight and usually dominant) leader. This will reduce the chances of a low weak fork developing. The second priority is to remove disproportionately large branches from the tree crown. A large branch is one that has a diameter greater than 50 % of the main stem diameter at the point of intersection with the main stem. If there are a number of these branches then the priority is to remove those lowest on the bole, up to a maximum of five large branches annually. Ideally, branches removed in formative pruning should not be allowed to become too large to cut with a knife or a pair of secateurs; early intervention will prevent large wounds which can allow defects and decay to develop.

The treatment should be started soon after establishment, and ideally continued annually until the objective of a single straight stem of at least 5 m in height is satisfied. If the cost of treating all trees is prohibitive resources should be concentrated on trees that are likely to be the final crop. A smooth cut wound can be produced using a sharp pruning knife or a pair of secateurs.

References

Williamson, D.R. and Lane, P.B. (1989). *The use of herbicides in the forest.* Forestry Commission Field Book 8. HMSO, London.
Williamson, D.R. (1992). *Herbicides for farm woodland and short rotation coppice.* Forestry Commission RIN 201. The Forestry Authority.

4 Natural regeneration

This chapter aims to give practical guidance on the natural regeneration of broadleaved woodlands. Silvicultural systems are described which can be used to achieve natural regeneration. However, it should be noted that some of these systems are equally applicable to artificial regeneration (planting). Where the production of quality timber is the main objective natural regeneration should only be pursued if the parent crop has good form and vigour and is well suited to the site.

Plate 27 Advance regeneration of oak.

(37238)

- Natural regeneration is often perceived as a system requiring great skill and art, but this is rather a misconception. The chances of success can be enhanced by following basic principles. If failure still ensues then trees can be planted.

- Plan for natural regeneration well in advance, about 20 years, thin to favour best trees and encourage large crowns for maximum seed production.

- Be flexible over marketing so that felling for natural regeneration coincides with a mast year. The period since the last seed year and observations of flowering in April–June will help predict the possibility of a good seed crop in the autumn.

- During or just after seedfall the forest floor should be cultivated to create a seedbed and the seed covered with mineral soil; competing vegetation should be controlled.

- A proportion of the overstorey should be removed after seedfall and before germination.

- Natural regeneration should be secured by protecting it from browsing and controlling competing weeds.

- Subsequent fellings should be timed so that the growth of natural regeneration is not impaired.

Artificial or natural regeneration?

Table 4.1 compares various aspects of artificial regeneration (planting) and natural regeneration. The former is necessary on new planting sites or on restock sites, if a change of species or provenance is required, or it is essential to achieve rapid and complete restocking. Natural regeneration has not been widely practised by British foresters because it requires a different style of management from that to which they have been accustomed. Natural regeneration requires flexibility by the grower to alter management plans to take advantage of natural regeneration when it occurs. This will mean premature or delayed felling to coincide with good seed years. The method may be favoured if the following conditions exist.

- The species and quality of the parent crop is satisfactory.

- There is evidence of good regeneration taking place and an opportunity to use it.

- There is no urgency to fell and regenerate in any one year.

- Conservation of local genetic stock is important.

Silvicultural systems

A silvicultural system may be defined as:

The process by which the crops constituting a forest are tended, removed and replaced by new crops, resulting in the production of stands of distinctive form.

In Europe there are many systems but in Britain attention can be confined to three: clear cutting, the group system and the shelterwood system.

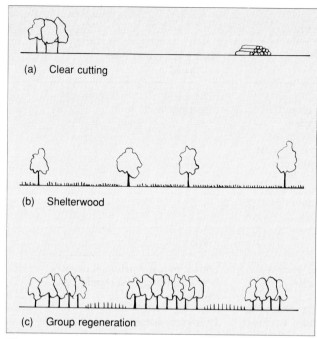

Figure 4.1 Diagrammatic representation of the main natural regeneration systems.

Clear cutting

Clear cutting (Figure 4.1(a)) has been the traditional system of regenerating broadleaved high forest in Britain. Large scale clearfelling is not widely practised and coupe sizes are now usually in the region of 1–3 ha. Complete removal of the crop exposes the soil surface, encourages weed growth, increases surface wetness and on heavy clay soils can lead to re-wetting (page 24). Clear cutting is usually followed by replanting because natural regeneration over areas of 1–3 ha rarely produces adequate stocking. The winged seeds of ash and sycamore are dispersed by the wind and have a greater chance of regenerat-

ing over such areas compared with the heavy seed of oak and beech. Where natural regeneration occurs it may be used in the following ways:

- If there is sufficient stocking of potential timber trees, these can be favoured by weeding and cleaning; filling in any gaps with planting or recruiting coppice regrowth.

- If the regeneration consists mainly of less valuable species, the woody regeneration can be used to provide side shelter for planted trees of a desired species and provenance.

Shelterwood

The shelterwood system (Figure 4.1(b)) involves partially felling a stand to leave a scattered overstorey of mature trees (the parent crop); regeneration then takes place in the shelter of the parent crop. Planting is usually used only to supplement areas where natural regeneration has failed. In Britain the system has been little used; however, under the right conditions it can succeed, and is particularly suitable for heavily seeded species such as oak and beech.

The group system

The group system (Figure 4.1(c)) is a widely used system for regenerating broadleaved high forest in Britain and is becoming increasingly important. It involves working on several small areas (0.1 to 0.5 ha) in the stand being regenerated. Once a new crop becomes established in the areas that were felled the groups are enlarged (say after 5 years) and new ones are also created. This approach does not depend on only one good mast year but allows a gradual regeneration process. The small scale of working will usually be more expensive, but there are considerable silvicultural gains because of the protected site.

Table 4.1   Comparison of natural regeneration with planting

		Natural regeneration	Artificial regeneration (planting)
1.	As a management practice	The existence of many complex European systems has given rise, in part, to perceived obstacles. However, British conditions are different and if attention is focused on real problems, e.g. timing of felling with mast years and protection against rabbits and deer, the method could be more successful in this country	Simple and reliable with good management
2.	Source of seed	The parent crop	Seed stand
3.	Seedlings	Arise freely on site and possess good shoot/root ratios and early vigour	Subject to many potential dangers before planting. Cost should be considered
4.	Stocking	Often patchy but provided stockings equivalent to planting are achieved a satisfactory stand should result	Uniform if managed properly
5.	Timing		
(a)	Felling previous crop	Determined by good seed years especially for oak and beech unless plentiful advance regeneration is present	Any time
(b)	Year of establishment	Usually a period of time following good seed years	Replanting can be done in any year provided plants are available
(c)	Season of planting	Not applicable	Autumn or early spring
6.	Genetics	Thinning leading up to regeneration must favour the best trees as parents of the new crop. No opportunity for species change. Dense regeneration allows greater selection of crop trees	New species or provenance can be introduced. Wide spacing, e.g. 3 m, provides limited choice for final crop

Plate 28 Ash. (39646)

Plate 29 Beech. (39645)

Plate 30 Sycamore. (39647)

Plates 28–30 Seed crops can be assessed
in the summer before seedfall.

Preparation for natural regeneration

The silvicultural essentials for satisfactory regeneration are plentiful seed, a clean forest floor, adequate protection and good weed control during the regeneration period.

Advanced regeneration

Advanced regeneration can often be found in stands producing fertile seed, most commonly under gaps in the canopy caused by uneven thinning, windthrow or along rides. If a stand is to be regenerated the areas of advance regeneration should be used as focal points for felling.

The parent crop

The objective in preparing the parent crop for natural regeneration is to ensure that the best trees are most likely to bear large quantities of seed. Selection of the best trees occurs throughout the rotation by selective silvicultural thinning; crown thinnings should be used in the latter part of the rotation to encourage larger crowns with greater seed-bearing capacity.

The importance of waiting for a good seed year cannot be overemphasised, especially for oak and beech which do not bear large quantities of seed every year. An assessment of the developing seed crop can be made using binoculars from ground

Plate 31 A disc plough suitable for the preparation of mineral soil during seedfall in a beech stand.
(M.J. POTTER)

Table 4.2   Seed production of broadleaved trees in Britain

Species	Minimum seed-bearing age (years)	Average interval between heavy seed crops (years)	Age after which seed production begins to decline (years)	Time of seedfall or seed dispersal (months)
Ash	15–20	3–5	80	Sep–Mar
Beech	40–50	5–15	160	Sep–Nov
Cherry	10	1–3	80	Jul–Aug
Oak				
pedunculate	40–50	3–6	180	Nov
sessile	40–50	2–5	180	Nov
Sweet chestnut	30–40	1–4	60	Oct–Nov
Sycamore	25–30	1–3	70	Sep–Oct

Note: Both rapidly growing trees and ones of coppice origin tend to bear seed earlier than shown. Decline in seed production is not a sudden event and heavy crops can occur, though with less regularity, well past 200 years of age for oak and beech.

level in late June (July and early August for sweet chestnut). Patterns of seed production in the principal broadleaved species are given in Table 4.2.

A good seed crop does not necessarily produce natural regeneration. Seed can lie dormant in the soil, e.g. ash for up to 18 months after seedfall.

Treatment of forest floor

The condition of the forest floor is critical for good germination and early survival of seedlings. Compacted, eroded or waterlogged soils are generally inhospitable to germination and in these circumstances cultivation or drainage may be required.

The grower can significantly improve the success of natural regeneration by:

- ensuring a seedbed of loosened mineral soil;
- removal of competing vegetation.

If these are achieved before seedfall, i.e. in late summer, then the seed will become covered by leaf litter throughout the autumn, creating ideal conditions for germination. Scarification or disc ploughing are the best methods of preparing a loosened mineral soil and there is some merit in doing this during or just after seedfall to incorporate some of the seed into the soil. Control of competing vegetation can be achieved by use of herbicides. The seed of some species such as ash can lie dormant in the soil for months, so patience may be required. Not infrequently good regeneration of these species has been observed 18 months after the original seedfall and the poor impression of the first year proved misleading. Figure 4.2 is a chronology of events for natural regeneration.

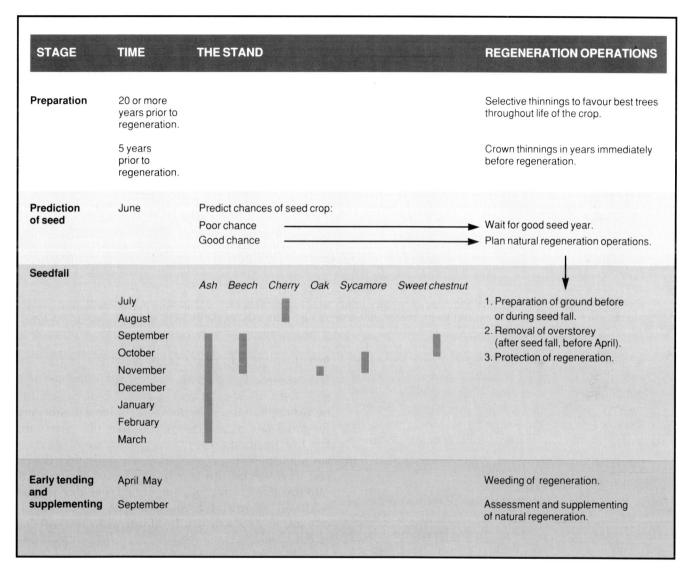

Figure 4.2 Chronology of events for natural regeneration.

Removal of the parent crop

The first stage in removing the parent tree should occur in the winter after seedfall; timber must be extracted before the following April. The question of which trees to fell, how many and the timing of removals is dependent on the silvicultural system employed and the light requirements of the species regenerating (the latter are outlined in Table 4.3). Manipulating the density of the canopy can be an effective way of controlling weeds on the site and also protecting against drought, frost and sun scorch. Removing too much will lead to prolific weed growth and greater susceptibility to frost, etc.; too little opening of the canopy will retard seedling germination and growth. Some species can tolerate low light levels when seedlings, despite being light demanding when older (e.g. oak and ash). Hence a balance must be found to permit sufficient levels of light to allow germination, balanced by the need to retain some overhead cover for protective functions and weed control.

The following guidelines may be useful:

For group system A minimum group felling should have a diameter of at least twice the height of adjacent trees.

For shelterwood For oak, ash and sycamore, leave at least 6 m between the remaining crowns. For beech the gap size may be reduced to 4 m. The remaining trees should be distributed uniformly over the site; their value is mainly for weed control and protection.

Subsequent fellings

The timing of these is critical: failure to remove trees at the appropriate time can seriously harm the progress of regeneration.

For group system After 4–5 years two operations are carried out:

1. enlargement of the group is essential once seedlings are established;
2. new groups are opened and old ones enlarged when the next good seed year occurs.

The number of trees to be removed should be chosen according to silvicultural criteria.

For shelterwood Ash, cherry, sycamore, sweet chestnut: complete removal of the overstorey in 3 to 4 years.
Oak: removal over 5 to 7 years in two operations.
Beech: removal over 15 to 20 years is possible because of the shade tolerance of beech.

Felling operations

Felling is part of any managed regeneration process and opportunities to benefit the site and minimise damage to the crop should be taken. Extraction of logs over the site is one method of scarifying and incorporating seed into the ground. Seedlings of the regeneration are damaged surprisingly little by felling except when frosted, which renders them brittle and liable to snap, making it inadvisable to fell or extract in cold frosty weather. In general fell into areas of very dense regeneration.

Plate 32 Group regeneration of beech.

Table 4.3 Light requirements for regeneration

Species	Remarks
Ash	Moderately shade tolerant but within 3–4 years requires full overhead light for satisfactory growth
Beech	Shade tolerant throughout life but do not protect with dark coloured treeshelters, clear or white are best
Cherry	As for ash
Oak	Light demanding throughout life: some evidence that sessile will stand more shade than pedunculate
Sycamore	Generally more tolerant of shade than ash
Sweet chestnut	As for ash

Protection of regeneration

The requirements to protect natural regeneration from climatic damage, mammals and weeds, are mostly similar to those for artificial regeneration. However, there are differences.

- Browsing by small animals, rabbits and deer constitute the most widespread danger to regeneration: every effort should be made to control it (see Chapter 5).

- Brambles can damage young seedlings if they are too dense, by shading out or preventing straight growth. However, if they appear at the same time as regeneration and do not become too dense too quickly, they can protect seedlings against browsing animals and frost.

- Oak regeneration under its own canopy is sometimes less profuse than may be expected but is not impossible.

- If treeshelters are used they should be placed over the young trees by early September of their first year, the aim being to protect at least 1100 trees per hectare. Individual tree protection is usually the best method with the group system because it allows flexibility when enlarging groups.

- In shelterwood and group systems where some shade is cast on the regeneration only transparent or white treeshelters should be used: this is particularly important for beech.

Figure 4.3 is a guide to the identification of young natural regeneration.

Supplementing regeneration

Stocking should first be assessed in early autumn of the first or second year after regeneration has begun. Any gap larger than about 7 m x 7 m should be planted. This allows opportunity to modify the species balance. Recruiting coppice is an efficient way of supplementing stocking; stools should be thinned down to one or two shoots per stool at the time of cleaning or respacing. Suckering is a feature of cherry and can occur up to 10 m from the parent stem, providing an additional method of supplementing regeneration.

Cleaning and respacing

The cleaning requirements of natural regeneration do not differ from those of plantations but the operation is more important; unwanted woody growth, including coppice and climbers, must not be allowed to threaten the desired crop. However, often the operation is combined with respacing where dense regeneration is thinned to prevent the intense competition producing thin, weak stems.

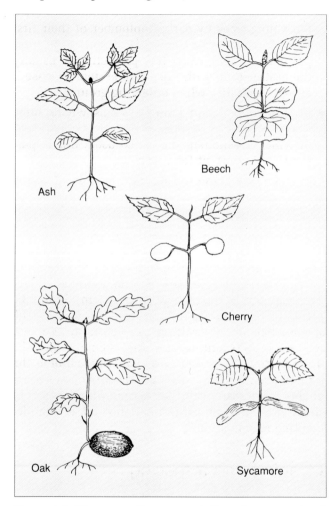

Figure 4.3 Diagrammatic representation of young natural regeneration of the principal broadleaves. Note the shape of the cotyledons (seed leaves) and first true leaves. The cotyledons are distinctive for each species and the first true leaves are often a different shape to mature leaves.

Cleaning and respacing should begin once regeneration is about 2 m tall. At this stage the vigour of bramble is declining and some side branches are being suppressed. Delay, especially for ash and sycamore, can be very injurious and ruin an otherwise promising crop. It is not adequate simply to let individuals compete for superiority, i.e. an early self-thinning, since this selects only for vigour and not stem form. Where regeneration is thick respacing should be done lightly, for example, reducing stocking from 50 000 trees to 10 000 trees per hectare on the first occasion and to more normal levels of 2500 to 3500 trees per hectare, 2 or 3 years later, when trees have reached about 3m average height. Frequent light cleanings/respacings are preferable to one heavy one. Investment in such cleaning and respacing is essential and rewarding but along with much more careful weeding leads to considerable expense. Satisfactory establishment of a stand by natural regeneration often requires a larger investment than for artificial regeneration. There are two possible ways of reducing costs by treating a proportion of the crop.

1. **Rack cutting.** This is commonly used in Denmark, France and Germany. Parallel racks, 1 m wide, are cut every 12–16 m (n) through the regeneration at an early age. Cleaning and respacing is then carried out 3–4 m ($\frac{1}{4}n$) on both sides of the rack, so that roughly only 50% of the crop is treated. The racks improve access and so reduce the cost of respacing, while dividing the stand for management purposes.

2. **The Garfitt method.** Cleaning and releasing of 2 stems (>2 m apart), to develop to pole size, at approximate intervals of 7–8 m through the stand. Each favoured tree is cleared to a distance of 1.2 m radius and the intervening matrix is untouched.

5 Protection

The protection of broadleaved woodland is a vital part of the overall management strategy when the primary objective is growing quality timber. The woodland is in danger from a large number of damaging agents whose pattern of attack, timing and degree of possible damage show considerable variation. The grower must be aware of the danger posed by mammals, pests and diseases and decide on cost-effective protection measures.

Mammals

Damage from mammals is the most important aspect of protection to consider with the main objective of growing quality broadleaved timber. The woodland provides a variety of habitats offering food and shelter to deer, squirrels, rabbits, hares and voles. The population of rabbits in some areas has returned to pre-myxomatosis levels, roe and fallow deer continue to increase their range in the lowlands of Britain and the grey squirrel is not yet being effectively controlled over large areas. These mammals can all cause serious damage by browsing, bark stripping or fraying.

Failure to protect a vulnerable woodland during the regeneration phase can result in an extension of the costly establishment period, inadequate stocking or in extreme circumstances, replanting. Bark stripping on the main stem, which usually occurs later in the rotation can kill branches or whole trees and hence degrades timber quality by causing uneven growth and by allowing access to staining and rotting organisms; the ultimate result of this may be

ADVICE FOR SUCCESS

- In Britain a high standard of protection is essential for growing quality broadleaves.
- The choice of fencing or individual tree protection against mammals requires careful consideration.
- Control of grey squirrels in the vulnerable period of 10–40 years is crucial to growing quality broadleaves. An effective and economical method is warfarin poisoning using bait in hoppers: this should be used wherever it is legally permitted.

windsnap. Protection against mammals is therefore essential.

The likelihood of damage occurring can be assessed if information is available on the following.

- The status of the local population: is it declining or increasing? The best sources of information are local foresters, rangers or pest control groups.
- The capacity of the woodland to support the pest population; this requires knowledge of the habitat preferences of the pest and of crop susceptibilities.
- Observation and assessment of the occurrence of damage in the locality.

Plate 33 Bark stripping of beech by grey squirrel. (37279)

Plate 34 Warfarin-treated bait dispersed from hoppers provides effective control. (25718)

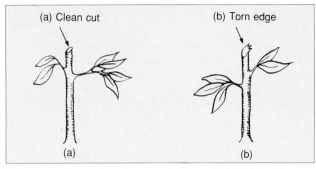

Figure 5.1 Browsing damage: (a) by rabbit, (b) by deer.

Identification of damage

It is easiest to identify damage when it is fresh so that the time of injury and the important diagnostic features can be observed. The differences between two damaging agents can sometimes be subtle, for instance browsing rabbits generally eat the shoots they bite off young trees (Figure 5.1(a)), whereas hares do not. If time has elapsed between damage and identification the severed shoots left by the hare may have disappeared, leading to a possibly false deduction.

All mammals referred to, except hares, strip bark from trees and identification of the culprit can be difficult. As an aid, descriptions of the teeth pattern left when biting or stripping are given in Table 5.2. However, positive identification requires fresh damage and a good eye. Other signs of the presence of animals, such as droppings, footprints, runs, and their abundance should also be taken into account.

Damage occurs in three main ways.

- **Browsing** This is the removal of buds, shoots and leaves for food (see Figure 5.1). It is rarely lethal but the most serious damage is removal of the leading shoot which can result in depressed height growth and multiple stems. Table 5.1 gives detailed descriptions of damage.

Table 5.1 Browsing damage

Mammal	Description of damage	Time of year
Deer: red, roe, fallow, sika and muntjac	Lack of teeth in front upper jaw produces a ragged edge on damaged stems (see Figure 5.1(b)). All species browse to a height of 1.1 m, fallow and red browse up to 1.8 m	Mid-November to spring (red: May/June)
Rabbits	Sharp angled cut on the ends of stems or branches which are bitten (see Figure 5.1(a)); these are then eaten. Damage occurs at any height up to 50 cm: higher in times of deep snow	Winter/spring occasionally summer
Hares	As rabbits but shoots are not consumed. Damage can be above 50 cm	As rabbits

- **Bark stripping** This is the removal of bark and underlying tissues with the incisor teeth. It most often occurs later in the rotation than browsing and can affect stem form and timber quality. Table 5.2 gives detailed descriptions of damage and crop susceptibilities.

- **Fraying** This is the removal of bark from the stems and branches of young trees by male deer rubbing the velvet from their new antlers or marking in preparation for the rut. The main fraying period for roe deer is March to August and for other lowland species from mid-July to mid-September.

Table 5.2 Bark stripping damage

Mammal	Species	Size/age	Description of damage	Time of year
Grey squirrel	Beech and sycamore are most susceptible but all tree species can be damaged	10 to 40-year-old trees	Bark stripping is most serious on the stem but can occur on root spurs or branches; the latter is most likely to occur in trees older than 40 years when the main stem bark is too thick. Incisor marks are 1.5 mm wide in pairs, running parallel along branches and vertically on stems	May to mid-August
Rabbits	All affected. Thin barked species such as ash and sycamore are most susceptible	All	Bark stripping can occur on root spurs and lower stems up to a height of 50 cm Incisor marks are 3–4 mm wide, in pairs, usually running diagonally across the stem Easily confused with squirrel damage if time of attack is unknown	Winter to early spring
Deer	All	Thicket and early pole stage	Method of bark stripping produces characteristic 'stripped wallpaper' appearance. The lower incisor is used to bite into the tree, the bark then pulled upwards leaving vertical teeth marks at the base of the wound Width of teeth mark 6.4 mm; maximum height of teeth marks 1.1 m	January to early spring
Field voles	All	Young trees up to 5 cm in diameter	Bark is stripped on the roots or lower stem up to the height of surrounding vegetation from where the attack is carried out. Very small trees can be girdled and felled Bark is usually removed in irregular strips 5–10 mm wide; incisor marks 1 m wide in pairs	All year, but greatest risk when food is in short supply, i.e. winter
Bank voles	All	As above	As above but will climb, causing damage up to 3 m from ground. Less common than field vole damage	As above
Edible dormouse[a]	Beech	10 to 40-year-old trees	Confined to crown, bark stripped in short lengths usually girdling the tree	June/July

[a] Protected species confined to Chilterns area.

Table 5.3 Protection against mammals

Mammal	Individual tree protection	Fencing	Other
Fallow deer	Must be at least 1.8 m high	Fence to 1.8 m or 2 m	Control by annual culling
Roe deer, Muntjac	Must be at least 1.2 m high	Fence to 1.8 m	Control by annual culling (see Ratcliffe and Mayle, 1992)
Rabbits	At least 0.6 m high	Fence to height of 0.75 m or 0.9 m, bottom 15 cm buried towards rabbits and secured by pegs or turfs	A land owner is legally required to control rabbits if present. Gassing from October to mid-March is most effective
Hares	At least 0.75 m high	Fence height either 0.75 or 0.9 m; 0.7 m fencing is ineffective	
Voles	20–30 cm tall (above height of surrounding vegetation), buried at least 5 mm into soil	Supplementary vole guards are advisable in fenced areas if weed control is not meticulous	Maintenance of weed-free area 1 m diameter around each tree will reduce incidence and severity of damage
Grey squirrel	n/a	n/a	Poisoning in April to July
Edible dormouse	n/a	n/a	Protected species: live trapping only permissible under licence from MAFF

Protection

There are two essential elements in any protective strategy for broadleaved woodland:

1. The regeneration phase, a decision to use fencing or individual tree protection.
2. Control of grey squirrels.

Fencing or individual tree protection

The choice between individual tree guards and fencing is dependent on the area to be protected and the number of planted trees per hectare. In general terms individual tree protection is normally more economical on areas less than 1 to 2 ha. If treeshelters are the chosen method of individual tree protection they confer additional benefits (page 27); these are difficult to cost but should be considered in any decision. Table 5.3 and Figure 5.2 give more detail on the specifications of each method of protection and other supplementary control measures. Fencing specification in terms of height and mesh size must form an adequate barrier against animals to be

Plate 35 Beech bark disease. (26810)

excluded (Table 5.4). Plain line wire fences are less effective than when supported by wire mesh. The durability of the materials used must be sufficient to last until the trees are well established.

Grey squirrels

Control of bark stripping damage to trees by grey squirrels is most effectively and economically achieved by poisoning with 0.02% warfarin on wheat dispensed from hoppers. The use of warfarin is prohibited in Scotland, and some counties of England and Wales and wherever red squirrels are present; in these areas spring or cage trapping should be used. A recently approved hopper modification has greatly reduced the risk of poisoning non-target birds and mammals (see Figure 5.3).

Hoppers should be placed at the base of trees in early April at a density of 1 per 3 to 5 ha. This area relates to the total area protected and not just most susceptible crops in the age range 10–40 years. Unpoisoned yellow maize is scattered around the tunnel entrance when the hoppers are first put out, to draw squirrels down to feed from these dispensers. To be effective there must be a constant supply of poison bait available in the hoppers until the end of the control season in late July.

In 1985, as part of the policy on broadleaved woodlands, the Forestry Commission proposed the formation of regional grey squirrel control groups. Their main functions were envisaged to be the co-ordination of control throughout an area, training and recruiting new members. The formation of such groups is the best way to achieve control on the scale required; however, only a small number have been established.

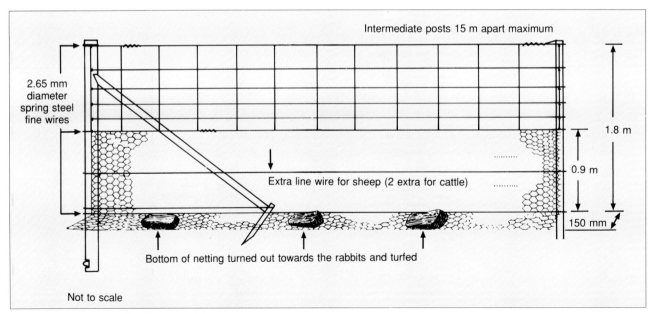

Figure 5.2 A deer and rabbit proof fence.

Table 5.4 Deer fence and woodwork specifications

Woodwork sizes

	Length (m)	Top diameter (cm)
Red, sika or fallow deer		
End posts	2.8	12–18
Struts	2.5	10–13
Stakes	2.6	8–10
Roe deer		
End posts	2.8	10–13
Struts	2.5	8–10
Stakes	2.5	5–8

Wire mesh types and patterns

Type	Pattern	
	Roe	Fallow, red and sika
Top mesh		
Hexagonal	75 mm x 900 mm x 19 gauge	
Welded	FF13	FF3 FF5 FC2 FC3
Woven		C8/80/30, C6/90/30 HT8/80/30
Bottom mesh		
Hexagonal	31 mm x 1050 mm x 18 gauge	31 mm x 1050 mm x 18 g plus two extra line wires
Welded	FF13 FF1	FF1 FC1
Woven	C7/10/15 C8/80/15	C8/80/15, C7/10/15 HT8/80/15

HT16/180/30

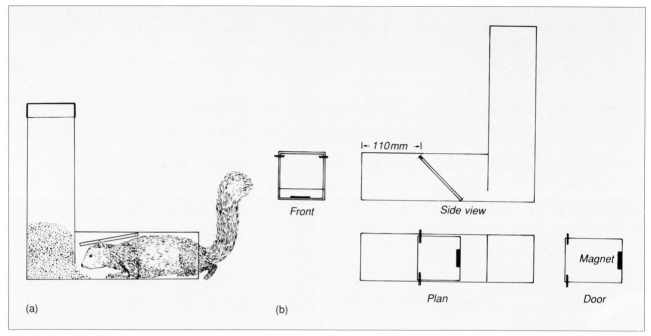

Figure 5.3 A modified squirrel hopper: (a) in action, (b) views and dimensions.

Pests and diseases

The most effective insurance policy a grower can employ against pests and diseases is to practise good forestry. Although there are a few insects and fungi which cause more damage on vigorous trees than unhealthy ones, it is a good general rule that a tree that is growing well on a suitable site will be better placed to withstand the effects of pests and diseases than one which is ill-suited to its locality. During regeneration, which is arguably the time of greatest vulnerability, good pre-planting and establishment practice outlined in this Handbook should ensure that problems are minimized. The prevention of mechanical damage such as bark stripping will deny some potentially dangerous organisms access to the trees.

Broadleaved tree species are particularly rich in insects, invertebrates and fungi. Many of these are harmless and many are held in ecological balance by natural predators. For instance, oak and willow support between them more than 850 species of insect and yet rarely suffer serious damage. It can be argued that the recuperative ability of broadleaved trees makes them better able to cope with the problems posed by pests and diseases than coniferous species.

The diagnosis of the cause of damage is complicated by the wide variety of possible agents. As well as organisms such as fungi and insects, these

Plate 36 Fruit bodies of *Armillaria* (honey fungus) around a dead elm stem.

(27619)

57

Table 5.5 Serious diseases and pests

Species	Disease/pest	Damage signs and symptoms	Comments and possible control measures
Ash	Ash canker Bacterium *Pseudomonas savastanoi* or the fungus *Nectria galligena*	Stem distorted with sunken cavities: wood may become stained or rotted	Remove diseased trees in thinning operations
	Large pine weevil *Hylobius abietis*	Kills young trees. Adult strips bark and girdles stem	Only a problem if conifers have been recently felled locally. Pre- or post-planting application of insecticide (see page 60)
Beech	Beech bark disease A weakly parasitic fungus *Nectria coccinea* that may follow attack by felted beech coccus, *Cryptococcus fagisuga*	Dark weeping 'tarry spots' on the bark indicate fungal attack (usually only on trees heavily infested by beech coccus). Minute globular red fruit bodies of *Nectria* may sometimes be seen	The disease causes some mortality in 20 to 40-year-old plantations; sufficient trees usually survive to the final crop. Salvage badly affected stems by thinning, but only if economic
	Beech woolly aphid *Phyllaphis fagi*	Woolly colonies usually on undersides of leaves in May; browning of foliage	Particular problem in treeshelters, but no insecticide approved for use on planted trees. Ensure nursery stock is free of eggs
	Large pine weevil *Hylobius abietis*	See above	See above
Cherry	Cherry canker *Pseudomonas syringae*	Sudden branch dieback occurs. Young trees may die. Gum often exudes from bark	Control can be achieved by annual spraying but this is unlikely to be economic or acceptable. Use cherry as a small component of planting schemes
	Silver leaf disease *Chondrostereum purpureum*	Progressive death of branches sometimes leads to death of tree. The wood is stained brown and leaves may assume a silvery or leaden appearance. Small leathery brackets with purple underside form on dead wood	Pruning should be done only in June to August, using techniques outlined on page 67

Table 5.5 **Serious diseases and pests** *(continued)*

Species	Disease/pest	Damage signs and symptoms	Comments and possible control measures
Cherry *(continued)*	Honey fungus *Armillaria* spp.	Young trees die. White sheets of mycelium occur in cambium of dead roots or stem base. Honey coloured toadstools are formed	Avoid large concentrations of cherry when restocking old woodland sites
	Large pine weevil *Hylobius abietis*	See above	See above
Oak	Stem rot caused by *Stereum gausapatum* or *Laetiporus sulphureus*	Decay becomes visible following branch breakage, etc. Pale yellow brackets of *L. sulphureus* are often conspicuous on exposed decayed wood	Correct pruning practice should be followed, see page 67
	Oak mildew *Microsphaera alphitoides*	White bloom on leaves and shoot, which show distortion and poor growth	Usually a nursery pest but can attack oak natural regeneration and young coppice and older trees. In nurseries spraying with colloidal sulphur gives good control
	Oakleaf roller moth *Tortrix viridana* Winter moth *Operophtera brumata*	Trees are badly defoliated in early summer	Recovery is usually good although loss of increment may occur. Spraying possible but is not economic or desirable
	Large pine weevil *Hylobius abietis*	See above	See above
Sweet chestnut	Ink disease *Phytopthora*	Trees and coppice stools die. Dead roots and adjacent soil may become blue-black	Usually occurs on wet soils. Improved drainage may help
	Large pine weevil *Hylobius abietis*	See above	See above
Sycamore	Large pine weevil *Hylobius abietis*	See above	See above

include non-living agents such as frost, winter cold, drought, waterlogging and nutritional deficiencies. It is for these reasons that diagnosis of the causes of damage should be carried out by a suitably qualified expert. The Forestry Authority Research Division offers an advisory service in pathology and entomology to woodland owners and enquiries should be directed to: Forest Research Station, Alice Holt Lodge, Wrecclesham, Farnham, Surrey GU10 4LH.

Once the problem has been correctly diagnosed the grower must consider what action, if any, can be taken. Table 5.5 lists some of the major pests and diseases attacking six broadleaved species and outlines management strategies.

General problems

There are few general problems for the principal broadleaved species; however, the large pine weevil (*Hylobius abietis*) and honey fungus (*Armillaria* spp.) both cause harm. The large pine weevil is restricted for most of its life cycle to conifers; however, when conifers are felled the presence of an increased number of conifer stumps, in which the weevils breed, can produce large increases in population. The adults will feed indiscriminately on young conifers and broadleaved trees in the locality of felling from early March to December. The weevils strip bark and girdle the stem, damage which is usually lethal. Susceptible plants may suffer damage for up to 6 years after felling of the previous crop.

A pre-planting or post-planting application of insecticide can provide protection during the vulnerable first year. Advice on active ingredients, dosage rates and safe methods of application should be sought from the Forestry Authority if either form of treatment is contemplated.

Honey fungus (*Armillaria* spp.), which can be so damaging when young conifers are planted on old

Plate 37 The large pine weevil, *Hylobius abietis*.

woodland sites, does not cause serious damage to five of the six species considered in this handbook. Cherry is susceptible but the problem can be minimised by restricting it to small components of any regeneration.

Reference

Ratcliffe, P.R. and Mayle, B. (1992). *Roe deer biology and management*. Forestry Commission Bulletin 105. HMSO, London.

6 Thinning and pruning

ADVICE FOR SUCCESS

- The main objective of thinning broadleaves is to improve the *quality* of the final crop.

- Thinning for quality will be greatly assisted if a pool of 250–350 potential final crop trees is permanently marked early on, by painted bands or spots. Trees may then be selected with reference to these.

- The main determinant of correct thinning practice in a broadleaved stand is the species; each species requires a different approach.

- Many conifer : broadleaved mixtures in Britain have been badly thinned or suffered neglect. Thinning is crucial to maintain the balance of the mixture and to ensure that the usually faster growing conifer does not dominate and adversely affect the growth or quality of the broadleaved component.

- Pruning should aim to create a clear stem to a height of 5–6 m on potential final crop trees. Pruning can have a significant effect on log quality, and consequently value; at spacings presently used in Britain it is probably an essential operation for the production of quality hardwoods.

Thinning

The main objective of thinning broadleaves is to improve the quality of the remaining crop and, in general, consideration of volume production will be secondary. The removal of trees from a stand increases the growing space available to those remaining and as a result their diameter growth is enhanced. Most broadleaved species are grown to diameter sizes determined by the market, and it may therefore be tempting to thin heavily to achieve the required sizes quickly. However, very heavy thinnings may have deleterious effects on the quality of the crop, e.g. epicormic shoots on oak or low heavy branching on sycamore or cherry. Hence, it is important to select a balanced thinning regime to achieve

Plate 38 Clumps of cherry are common in broadleaved forests: in this case early intervention to reduce to one or two stems would have been beneficial.   (5E 03/90)

the objective of growing quality timber; diameter growth should be maximised with as little reduction in stem quality as possible. This chapter recommends how best to achieve this balance for the principal broadleaved species. However, it must be emphasised that without adequate stocking levels (see Table 3.1) and crop protection the improvement in quality through thinning alone will be limited.

Table 6.1 Thinning type	
Thinning type	**Description**
Selective	Trees are removed or retained on their individual merits
1 Low	Trees are removed predominantly from the lower canopy, i.e. suppressed and sub-dominant trees. Later in the rotation, thinning in the upper canopy will release the better dominants
2 Intermediate	Removal of most suppressed and sub-dominant trees and opening the canopy by breaking up groups of competing dominant and co-dominants. A hybrid of low and crown thinning
3 Crown	Trees are removed predominantly from the upper canopy, i.e. dominants and co-dominants, to allow selected dominants freedom to grow rapidly
Systematic	Trees are removed according to a predetermined system which does not permit consideration of the merits of individual trees, e.g. line thinning

Objectives of thinning

1. To improve stand quality by removing poorly formed, defective, damaged and diseased trees (see page 17 for guidance on how to remove oaks prone to shake).

2. To ensure future increment is concentrated on the best formed trees.

3. To produce revenue.

4. To ensure satisfactory development of mixed stands by the timely removal of secondary species.

5. To prepare for natural regeneration (late in the rotation).

Thinning practice

Thinning practice comprises the following elements:

- Thinning type: how to select trees to be removed in successive thinnings.

- Thinning intensity: the rate at which volume is removed.

- Thinning cycle and timing: when to start thinning and the interval between successive thinnings.

Thinning type

The various types of thinning referred to in this Handbook are explained in Table 6.1. Systematic thinnings take no account of tree quality, and are only appropriate for broadleaves at the first thinning to create a system of racks which will ease future extraction or when removing lines in strip mixtures. Later thinnings must be selective in accordance with the species recommendations later in this chapter. Thinning for quality will be greatly assisted if a pool of potential final crop trees is identified early on and

Table 6.2 Final crop selection and stocking of major broadleaved tree species			
	Approximate number of potential final crop trees to select, mark and favour in early thinnings stems ha^{-1} : spacing (m)	**Normal final crop stocking stems ha^{-1} : spacing (m)**	**Normal rotation age (years)**
Ash	350 (5.3)	120–150 (9.2–8.2)	65–75
Beech	250 (6.3)	100–120 (10.0–9.1)	95–140
Cherry	250 (6.3)	140–160 (8.5–7.9)	50–70
Oak	200 (7.1)	60–90 (12.9–10.5)	120–160
Sycamore	350 (5.3)	140–170 (8.5–7.7)	60–70
Sweet chestnut	250 (6.3)	100–190 (10.0–7.3)	60–70

permanently marked by painted bands or spots. This pool should ideally contain between two and four times the number of final crop trees required (see Table 6.2) and should be marked after the first thinning. Selection of a pool of final crop trees is best done in winter when the condition of the upper stem and crown is easily seen. Before marking it is advisable to observe the variability that exists throughout the area; selection should then generally meet the following criteria, in order of priority.

1. Good stem form and freedom from defect on the lower bole (bottom 7 m).
2. Absence of deep forking in the crown which increases risk of storm damage and eventual loss of tree.
3. Good vigour: observe shoot extensions in a gap in the crown; make comparative judgements.
4. Freedom from defect in the upper stem and crown, e.g. squirrel damage.
5. Low incidence of epicormic shoots (in the case of oak).
6. Spacing, seeking an even distribution of selected trees: this should usually only come after the other criteria above are satisfied.

Thinning should aim to favour this pool of trees and the creation of well-balanced even crowns. Wolf trees, which are large coarse trees occupying much room in the canopy, must be removed in the first or second thinning. If left they will leave large gaps in the canopy when finally felled and the cutting and extraction of such trees can cause considerable damage. In later thinnings some of the originally favoured trees will be removed, as well as some being lost due to natural causes.

(a)

(b)

Plate 39 The ash (a) and sycamore (b) have been left too long before thinning: sycamore will usually recover more successfully than ash.

(39697 + 3K 05/90)

Thinning intensity

Thinning intensity is defined as the rate of volume removal. The overriding importance of stem quality in determining stand value has already been stressed and it is important to view any reference to volume in this context.

Two stages in the life of a broadleaved stand may be distinguished.

1. The first stage is the time up to the age of maximum mean annual volume increment (maximum MAI); the theoretical rotation age at which maximum annual yield is achieved (Edwards and Christie, 1980) and also indicates its yield class. The ages of maximum MAI for a range of species and yield classes are given in Table 6.3. Until about 5 years before this age the thinning intensity should be 70 % of crop yield class per year. Rollinson (1988) describes how to check the actual yield of thinning marked, to enable the marker to make any necessary modifications.

2. The second stage is after the age of maximum MAI. The average rate of volume increment has decreased and therefore the thinning intensity must be correspondingly reduced or the thinning cycle extended (see below).

Thinning cycle

The first thinning of broadleaves, particularly for ash, cherry and sweet chestnut, is crucial and must be punctual. For crops at 3 m spacing thinning should begin when the top height is about 10 m and basal area between 20 and 30 m^2 ha^{-1}. For closer spacing or if markets exist earlier, thinning is possible once top height is greater than 8 m.

The need for later thinnings can be judged subjectively in summer when the amount of crown overlap and the proportion of trees not present in the canopy can be seen. A more objective way is to determine the basal area per hectare and compare it to the recommended threshold basal areas, shown in Rollinson (1988).

The thinning cycle need not be a rigid number of years though excessive delays between thinnings should be avoided. Generally intervals between thinnings before age of maximum MAI are 5–10 years and 10–15 years past this age. The longer the interval between thinnings, the greater will be the volume of produce harvested at each thinning; this has economic advantages. However, the effects on the remaining trees are more drastic, e.g. increased exposure, stimulation of epicormic shoots and uneven ring width leading to seasoning and working problems. The silvicultural ideal for most broadleaved stands is thinning little and often.

Plate 40 Thinning in oak: note the paint banded potential final crop tree.   (E7042)

Species recommendations

Ash

Ash is a strong light demander and the trees require crowns continually free from competition to grow quickly and produce quality timber with between 4 and 16 rings per inch (25 mm). This is best achieved by frequent crown thinnings (see Table 6.1) to perpetuate a live crown over at least one-third the height of the tree. Once a tree is constrained and the crown becomes small it responds poorly to further thinnings: once neglected, ash stands rarely recover. Remove trees with ash canker at the earliest opportunity.

Beech

In beech more than in other species young stands of moderate quality can be much improved by thinning. Until a clean bole of 7 m is formed stocking should be kept high and light intermediate thinnings employed. After this, despite its shade tolerance, full crown development should be encouraged by moderate to heavy crown thinnings, but strongly favour good stem form over uniformity of spacing.

Beech remains responsive to thinning after a period of neglect; however, care is required in older stands (>100 years) with thin drawn up trees and small crowns. In the latter case anything but light low thinning can lead to sun scorch, dieback and poor health. This condition known as 'stand collapse' is common in mature and overmature Chiltern beech woods if suddenly exposed by heavy thinning. Regeneration is then the only sensible silvicultural option.

Cherry

Silvicultural advice throughout this Handbook has been to plant cherry as a small component with

Table 6.3 Ages of maximum mean annual increment

	Yield class				
	4	*6*	*8*	*10*	*12*
Ash	45	45	40	40	40
Beech	95	90	80	75	–
Oak	80	70	65	–	–
Sycamore	45	45	40	40	40
Sweet chestnut	95	90	80	75	–

These figures are from *Yield models for forest management* (Edwards and Christie, 1980). The figures are based on close initial spacings of 1.2–1.5 m: wider spacings will increase the age of maximum mean annual increment.

other broadleaved species. Thinning in mixed stands should aim to ensure that the crowns of potential final crop trees are unimpeded and will remain so until the next thinning. Cherry is responsive when freed from suppression until about 40 years, after which response to thinning is sluggish. The desirable regime of heavy thinnings to achieve large size timber on a short rotation must be supplemented by pruning.

Oak

The production of epicormic shoots is a significant problem when attempting to grow quality oak (see Harmer, 1992). Recommendations for thinning oak are based on a strategy for controlling epicormic shoots. This is considered in a special section 'growing quality oak' at the end of this chapter (page 70).

Sycamore

Sycamore is a moderate shade bearer which is best thinned heavily using crown thinnings from an early age. Under-thinned or neglected sycamore will recover successfully, certainly more readily than ash, and probably better than any other broadleaf except beech.

Sweet chestnut

Sweet chestnut is a fairly strong light demander. It should be thinned to the same prescription as ash. If crown vigour is lost, response to further thinnings will be slow. The timber produced is similar in many respects to oak but epicormic shoots are not a problem.

Thinning of mixtures

Conifer: broadleaved mixtures

Neglect or delay of thinning, particularly the first thinning, is a more serious problem in mixtures than in pure stands because in time the conifer will usually dominate the broadleaf. Light demanding conifers such as larch or pine have rapid crown expansion and coarse branching which will lead to early interference with the broadleaved species. Shade-tolerant species such as western hemlock and western red cedar will have less effect than larch or pine. Thinning is the method of controlling the influence of the conifer.

The principles of early selection of potential final crop trees, priority removal of wolf trees, and the timing and cycle of the thinnings are substantially the same as for pure stands. Thinning intensity should be determined according to the guidance in Rollinson (1988).

In conifer: broadleaved row mixtures the first thinning should usually remove the outer conifer row on the south side of the broadleaves if the species are in reasonable competitive balance, or both outer rows if the broadleaved species is becoming surpressed. The broadleaved element is normally selectively thinned and trees extracted using the racks in the conifer. In the second thinning any remaining adjacent conifer row is removed and the rest of the crop selectively thinned. Subsequently thinnings are wholly selective, with most of the remaining conifer being removed in the third thinning unless strips or bands are very wide, such as five rows or more.

Thinning in block or group mixtures is more difficult. Where there are broadleaved groups in a matrix of conifer, remove rows adjacent to broadleaved groups and thin these groups selectively. Identify one or preferably more potential final crop trees in each group to ensure a predominantly broadleaved final crop.

Broadleaved mixtures

Thinning mixtures of broadleaves is relatively straightforward, the guiding principle being to favour good stems of all suitable main crop species and to remove wolf trees early. Where intermediate yields of good quality cherry, sycamore and/or ash are sought from mixtures with beech and/or oak, some selection in early thinnings of both the short rotation and the long rotation species will be necessary.

Pruning

The objective of pruning is to improve timber quality. The removal of live and dead branches from the main stem ensures that further outward growth in the stem is clear of knots and the more clear timber in a log the higher the timber quality. To maximise

Plate 41 Marking thinnings in beech. (E7085)

Plate 42 Pruning pole stage oak. (E7045)

the amount of clear timber the operation is best begun while the trees are small. Suppression and shedding of branches occurs naturally in well-stocked stands and generally only a little pruning will be required.

Pruning is expensive and if carried out is gener-ally confined to branches of less than 5 cm diameter at base and eventually to a height of 5–6 m on final crop trees. This is usually performed in two 'lifts': the first to 3 m prior to first thinning, the second to 6 m before the second thinning. Pruning higher than this should be achieved in a number of lifts each of

Plate 43 Extraction of small thinnings for pulp. (E7112)

69

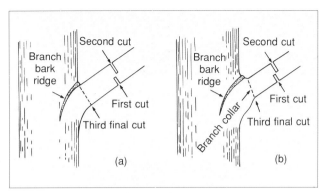

Figure 6.1 Diagram of 'natural' pruning position on a branch junction: (a) with no collar, (b) with collar.

3 m. To ensure no adverse effects on individual tree increment at least one-third of the total height of the tree should be crown. In the case of oak, special care is required to avoid exposing heartwood by pruning very thick branches as this may provide an entry point for fungi causing heart rot.

The best method of pruning is illustrated in Figure 6.1. The first stage is to remove most of the weight of the branch to ease the later cuts. This is achieved by a first undercut to prevent splitting, a second top cut then severs the branch at this point. Before the final cut is made the 'branch bark ridge' must be identified: this is an external feature which is readily visible at the trunk/bark junction (see Figure 6.1). The final cut must not disturb this ridge or the internal anatomical features associated with it.

The optimum time of pruning is a subject which is currently being studied by the Research Division of the Forestry Authority under contract to the Department of the Environment. Figure 6.2 indicates provisionally, for five of the principal broadleaves, the times of year when it is best to prune, e.g. cherry in July, and consequently times when it is inadvisable to prune have no shading, e.g. ash in December.

Growing quality oak

The importance of epicormic shoots in the silviculture of oak has already been noted. If they persist for more than 1 year on the stem a small knot is produced. For high quality timber such knots must be small and absent altogether for veneer. A strategy to control epicormic shoots must therefore form the basis of how to grow quality oak. Such a strategy will have two parts.

1. The prevention of emergence of the shoots: by planting species of oak less prone to epicormics and application of suitable thinning methods.

2. The prevention of epicormic shoots from becoming large branches: by encouraging an understorey of a shade-tolerant species supplemented by green pruning where necessary.

Species
There is some evidence that sessile oak has a lower incidence of epicormics than pedunculate oak. Where possible grow sessile oak.

Thinning
Sudden changes in stand density tend to result in the production of epicormic shoots. Frequent, light, intermediate thinnings will ensure balanced growth of potential final crop trees and avoid stress or overexposure of the crowns; these factors are crucial in avoiding epicormics. Additionally, trees with many epicormic shoots should be removed to favour those relatively free of them.

Understorey

To grow high quality oak the encouragement of an understorey of beech, hornbeam, small-leaved lime or hazel should be part of the overall silvicultural plan.

The shading effect of the understorey will not affect the initiation of epicormic shoots but will reduce their survival and vigour. This will prevent the formation of knots and thus improve quality and price of the end product.

The cost of planting such an understorey is prohibitive, though it is a common practice in Europe.

Pruning

Pruning epicormics is an expensive operation and should only be used to supplement the effects of the understorey. Shoots should be removed or rubbed off up to 7 m height in mid-season, preferably June. The time of most need will be before and after the time of first thinning, before the understorey is effective. Pruning should be carried out only on the pool of final crop trees. A chisel pruner is the usual tool. Research in the early 1980s (Evans, 1987) did not produce any chemical or mechanical method of epicormic control of sufficient reliability or cheapness; green pruning remains the only option.

SUMMARY OF RECOMMENDATIONS

In order of priority these are:

- Thin lightly and often, removing trees with epicormic shoots and favouring ones relatively free of them.

- Encourage an understorey of shade-tolerant species if they coppice or seed into the area.

- Green prune or rub off epicormics from potential final crop trees in June in the early part of the rotation and later supplement the effects of any understorey.

- Plant sessile in preference to pedunculate oak.

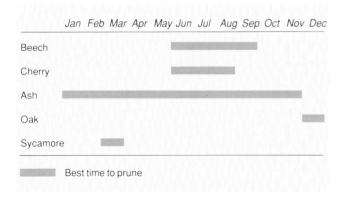

Figure 6.2 Time to prune.

References

Edwards, P. N. and Christie, J. M. (1980). *Yield models for forest management.* Forestry Commission Booklet 48. Forestry Commission, Edinburgh.

Evans, J. (1987). The control of epicormic branches. In *Advances in practical arboriculture,* ed. D. Patch. Forestry Commission Bulletin 65. HMSO, London.

Harmer, R. (1992). *Do dominant oaks have few epicormic branches?* Forestry Commission RIN 223. The Forestry Authority.

Rollinson, T. J. D. (1988). *Thinning control.* Forestry Commission Field Book 2. HMSO, London.

7 Harvesting and marketing

Harvesting

Rotation length

The market for hardwood timber is strongly determined by technical considerations especially log diameter and straightness. The lower diameter limits for most markets are fairly rigid; however, when supply is short and demand high, lower diameter limits may fall. Upper limits are more flexible and are usually determined by conversion equipment at the factory. This allows felling of large sized trees to be timed to silvicultural plans or market demand. The diameter specifications for various end uses are shown in Table 7.1.

With the emphasis on size it is difficult to specify precise rotation lengths to yield produce of particular sizes because of the influences of site, thinning and climate. However, for planning purposes estimates are given in Table 7.2, which indicate minimum rotation lengths by species and site fertility.

Harvesting practices

Harvesting broadleaves can be carried out by timber merchants to whom standing trees have been sold by specialist contractors who do some or all harvesting operations; or by directly employed workers. Modern timber harvesting requires competent planning and a high degree of operator skill: it is not a job for amateurs. Inadequately planned and poorly executed logging can reduce log quality and result in serious financial loss, and effectively wastes years of painstaking silviculture.

Plate 44 Extraction using a Timberjack skidder.

Table 7.1 Diameter specifications for various end uses

Product	Quality Class [a]	Diameter overbark (cm)					
		10	20	30	40	50	60+
Firewood	IV	———————————————————————————- - - - - - -					
Pulpwood	IV	———————————					
Turnery sycamore, ash, beech	III		————————- - - - - -				
Fencing (sawn) cleft/round	II	——————————- - - -					
Mining timber (sawn)	III			—- - - - - - - - - - - - - - - - - - -			
Prime timber planking/furniture/joinery high-class joinery	I			- ————————————- - - - - -			
Veneer ash/sycamore/sweet chestnut cherry oak	I+			- - - - - - - - - - - - - - - - - - - ————————————————————- - - ——————- -			
Miscellaneous sports ash	I+			——————- - - - - -			

[a] See Table 7.3.

The choice of who is to harvest timber and the method used can only be made according to local conditions and circumstances. However, irrespective of local factors the following principles generally apply to the harvesting of quality broadleaves.

1. The preferred time for felling is from autumn to early spring when the sap is down, so that the timber does not dry out too quickly after felling.

2. Inexpert felling can cause severe stem degrade; especially splitting of the stem. This is particularly serious in ash but all species are prone.

3. Directional felling should be used wherever possible. In thinnings this should aim to create the least possible damage to the remaining stand. Large size trees should not be allowed to impact directly on a large branch or hit uneven ground such as a gully or rock which may cause stem splitting. If possible, falling trees should be directed into the best areas of natural regeneration. However, if this is not possible log extraction should be along the line of fall to minimise damage.

4. In later thinnings or regeneration fellings, if ground skidding is used, valuable stems in the remaining crop should be protected against stem abrasion. This can be done by erecting posts near

Table 7.2 Minimum rotation lengths (years)

Species	Prime timber			Veneer	
	Site quality			Site quality	
	fertile	*average*	*poor*	*fertile*	*average*
Ash [a]	50	65	80	55	75
Beech	75	95	120	110	140
Cherry [b]	(50)	(65)		60	80
Oak	100	120	160	120	160
Sweet chestnut	45	60	75	50	70
Sycamore	45	60	75	55	70

Notes:
[a] Sports quality ash may be obtained on shorter rotations than shown.
[b] Cherry is rarely felled only for prime timber: though it can be used for high-class joinery, material is mostly obtained from trees felled for veneer.

to these trees along extraction racks, which need to be planned and marked in advance to minimise damage.

5. Wherever possible avoid extracting logs when ground conditions are very wet.

Marketing

Marketing is the process of determining demand for a product, motivating its sale and securing the best possible price for it. The actual sale is, therefore, only one element of marketing. Good timber marketing requires:

1. A sound knowledge of the timber parcel to be sold.

2. Knowledge of timber markets and how various factors influence price.

3. Good presentation of the timber parcel and accurate supporting documentation for prospective buyers.

The marketing of hardwood timber in Britain is relatively undeveloped compared with the marketing of softwoods. Softwoods are sold frequently, felled or standing, at periodical well-publicised auctions throughout the country, organised by the Regional Offices of Forest Enterprise, and results are published. Current market prices for different species and products are readily accessible to any interested party. With one or two exceptions this is not the case with hardwoods. Lack of current information on prices adds to the problems of marketing hardwood timber.

Knowledge of timber values requires an appreciation of local, regional and even national or international markets, both of price levels and current demand. Growers of quality hardwoods are advised to contact a professional consultant or a growers organisation for this information. They should offer the following benefits.

1. They will be able to grade timber and ensure that the best market prices are obtained. For example, the price differential between second quality and veneer oak can be a factor of ten; identification of the difference between shake and drying cracks in logs could be critical.

2. Wood characteristics such as 'brown oak' and 'curly grain' in sycamore are periodically fashionable in the furniture industry. Market information such as this could result in premiums being paid.

3. Knowledge of supply patterns from neighbouring estates may result in a cooperative approach to marketing. This has many potential benefits particularly for the small woodland owner.

4. Experience and advice on the best method of sale, point of sale and presentation of timber to potential buyers.

In general terms there is always a ready market for high quality timber and often a local demand for small diameter roundwood; however, as discussed in Chapter 1, special efforts will be needed to locate good markets for second quality logs. In an attempt to provide more information the Forestry Commission (1989) has published *County lists of mills, merchants and contractors* which currently covers England and Wales. The objective of these lists is to act as a link between growers or consultants who have timber to sell and people seeking to buy timber. These lists are available free from Publications Section, The Forestry Authority, Forest Research Station, Alice Holt Lodge, Wrecclesham, Farnham, Surrey, GU10 4LH. Information about merchants may also be found in the BTMA *Buyers' Guide to British Timber.*

Method of sale

There are three possible methods of sale: negotiation, tendering and auction. The relative merits of each are discussed.

Negotiation

Prices and other conditions of sale are agreed between buyer and seller and a suitable contract drawn up between them. Negotiated sales depend on the grower having a particularly good knowledge of timber value, including the merchant's probable markets and revenue, his costs and the amount he can be expected to be able to pay for the timber in consequence.

Plate 45 Delimbing a mature oak stem. (40233)

Plate 46 Felling a mature oak. High lift wedge provides essential directional control.

(40226)

Tender

Sales by tender are competitive and can generally be expected to give a true reflection of market prices. Tenders can be invited from selected merchants or by advertising in the trade press. The precise terms of sale must be determined before advertising, and copies sent to interested potential buyers so that they know exactly what these conditions are before tendering. This is necessary because acceptance of a tender automatically concludes a contract on the advertised or published conditions.

Auction

Opportunities for auctioning hardwood timber have been limited. These sales avoid the drawback of the tendering system, whereby a merchant can lose a parcel of timber because his tender is only marginally lower than the highest offer received and there is no chance to revise the price. Such an outcome could disrupt the merchant's working, resulting in possible inefficiency and lower prices being offered. Auctions attract interest from a wide range of buyers and can result in competitive prices being paid.

Choice of method

No one method of sale is best for all circumstances, and even the most experienced growers may find it advantageous to consult a growers' organisation to help decide which method of sale to use. This is particularly true of competitive sales, where careful timing and grouping of advertisements and advance warning of future sales are necessary to achieve maximum effect. There are also advantages to be gained by coordinating marketing efforts with neighbouring growers, so as to be able to offer larger and more concentrated volumes of timber in one locality. This enables growers, or merchants buying standing timber, to make the best use of harvesting resources, to negotiate better road haulage contracts, and be in a stronger selling position with regard to customers.

Point of sale

Standing sale

The sale of trees 'standing' to a timber merchant is relatively easy, involving the grower in minimal outlay, work and commercial risk. The grower also knows, before a tree is cut, what his financial return will be. The trees to be sold are either individually marked or the boundaries of the area to be worked are marked and the individual trees to be felled within that area are indicated in some way.

Each parcel should be described separately, giving estimated number of trees, estimated total volume, and estimated average volume per tree for each species. Recording the number of trees by breast height diameter classes, and calculating the total volume estimated for each class, is often helpful to both sides in arriving at the price to be paid.

The conditions under which the timber is to be sold should be clearly defined in a contract.

Felled sales

The sale of quality hardwood timber is usually conducted on felled logs to allow buyers to inspect for flaws such as shake and butt rot. The absence of any defects will probably ensure the best prices are paid for quality logs. Care must be exercised with ash, beech and sycamore because significant degrade will occur if logs are left in the wood.

Experience of marketing broadleaves

In 1987, before the gale of 16 October, a project was initiated by the Forestry Commission's Research Division to examine marketing of broadleaves. An important part of this was a survey, by questionnaire, of Timber Growers (UK) Limited members in England and Wales. The objective was to ascertain views on the quality and amount of wood they wished to market and any problems they foresaw. In all, 410 replies were received from all regions of England and Wales representing five yearly programmes of 100 to over 5000 m³.

Approximately one-third of replies indicated an intention to harvest volumes of between 1 and 199 m³ over the next 5 years, another third predicted volumes between 200 and 999 m³ (see Figure 7.1). The hardwood timber to be felled constituted 36 % oak, 18 % ash, 17 % beech and 10 % sycamore (see Figure 7.2).

The questionnaire requested information on the type of produce expected. Overall, the planned cut was expected to yield 33 % of first and better second quality roundwood, 15 % second quality (fencing), 20 % third quality (mining) and 32 % fourth quality (fuelwood and pulp or particle board roundwood). See Table 7.3 for more information on grading for quality (classes I–IV). Overall two-thirds of the volume were expected to be sold standing or at stump, although this proportion was less for the larger programmes.

One important question in the survey concerned problems experienced in selling timber in the period 1985–1987. Respondents were asked to express a priority for their reasons. The replies were analysed in terms of predicted harvesting programmes. Problems associated with price, small volumes and lack of buyers accounted for 60 % of the score for those with programmes of 1–199 m³, but only 37 % of those with programmes 1000–4999 m³. For those with the larger size of programme, 33 % concerned restrictions caused by outside interests.

For the largest programmes, that is over 5000 m³, difficulties in obtaining contractors and equipment became important, reaching 29 % of the score. A final but important result was that 21 % of respondents volunteered the information that they had no problem in selling timber; however, as might be anticipated this observation was less frequent for those with small programmes than those with large ones.

The main conclusion of the survey was that a significant factor in British hardwood marketing is the small-size holdings and the economic difficulties associated with these when marketing timber. This reinforces the recommendations (page 76).

- Before contemplating marketing hardwood timber contact a professional consultant or growers organisation.
- Co-operatives are a sensible solution to problems created by small scale of working.

The results of this survey are more fully reported by Thompson (1988).

Potential end uses

There are two factors that determine the potential end uses of broadleaved timber: the log size and the log quality.

1. Size: as mentioned earlier in this chapter the lower diameter limits for most markets are fairly rigid, but upper limits are more flexible. The diameter specifications for various end uses, as well as the quality demanded, are shown in Table 7.1.

2. Quality: the quality of a felled log can be determined according to external characteristics. The information in Table 7.3 is for the guidance of the grower only but allows logs to be classified into five grades which relate to their end uses. The following notes should be used in conjunction with Table 7.3.

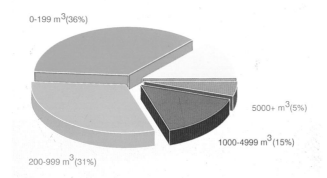

0-199 m^3(36%)

5000+ m^3(5%)

1000-4999 m^3(15%)

200-999 m^3(31%)

Figure 7.1 Marketing broadleaves: relative parcel sizes sold by TGUK members (1987–91).

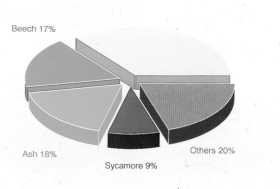

Beech 17%

Ash 18%

Sycamore 9%

Others 20%

Figure 7.2 Marketing broadleaves: species composition of harvesting volumes in Figure 7.1.

Plate 47 Presentation of a log parcel at roadside for sale by negotiation.

(40221)

Plate 48 Roadside grading of beech logs.   (E7781)

Plate 49 A fine oak stem being assessed for diameter at breast height.   (40504)

Table 7.3   Log quality classes

Log defects	Maximum permitted in each class				
	Class I+ [a]	*Class I*	*Class II*	*Class III*	*Class IV*
Sweep		None	Not greater than 10% of top diameter	Not greater than 20% of top diameter	Not greater than 30% of top diameter
Spiral grain	None	None	5 cm in 4 m	5 cm in 3.5 m	No restriction
Knot dimension (a) Sound knots, and clusters of epicormic branch knots	None	Up to 5 cm in diameter	Up to 7.5 cm in diameter	Up to 10 cm in diameter	No restriction
(b) Dead or decayed knots	None	None	None	Up to 5 cm in diameter	No restriction
Knot frequency (including clusters of epicormic branch knots)	None	One per 2 m run	One per 1.5 m run	No restriction	No restriction
Butt rot No other type of rot permitted	None	None	5% of diameter at butt	15% of diameter at butt	50% of diameter at butt
Blackheart	None	None	25% of diameter	50% of diameter	No restriction
Ring shake	None	None	None	Not occurring beyond 50% of the radius from the pith	No restriction
Star shake	None	None	None	Extending no further than 50% of radius from pith	No restriction
Position of pith	None	Well centred at both ends	Well centred at both ends	Reasonably central at both ends	Unspecified
'Worm' holes	None	None	None	None	No restriction

Based on *Log grades for hardwoods,* Princes Risborough, 1967.
[a] No defects permitted.

Sweep   The maximum deviation of the surface of a log measured perpendicular to a line joining the circumference at both ends and expressed as a percentage of the top diameter. When a log curves in two directions in one plane only (double sweep), the sum of the two maximum deviations, each measured as for single sweep, is expressed as a percentage of the top diameter (Figure 7.3). A sudden deviation of the axis of a log (single bend) is treated as sweep. Where sweep in two planes occurs, the secondary sweep shall not exceed 5 % of the top diameter in any grade.

Spiral grain   This is grain which follows a spiral course in one direction around the stem. It is often indicated by the pattern of the bark.

Knot dimension   This is the diameter of a knot when measured over its greatest width.

Epicormic branch   A branch that originates from a dormant bud on the trunk. A cluster of epicormic branch knots is treated as a single knot, the cluster diameter being treated as the diameter of a single knot. Permitted frequency of such clusters in any grade is as for single knots.

Butt rot   Seen on the lower end of the butt log, this is permitted as shown in Table 7.3.

Blackheart   This is measured when visible on cross-cut ends. Where blackheart is seen at the butt of a felled tree which is to be graded without cross-cutting, the grader shall make allowance, based on experience, for the possibility of its affecting lengths other than the butt log.

Position of pith   Where there is doubt as to the degree of eccentricity of the pith as seen on a cross-cut end, the allowances in Table 7.4 apply.

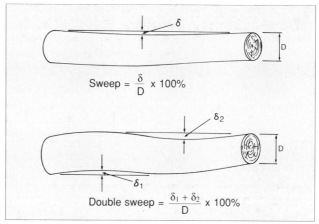

Figure 7.3 Measurement of sweep for hardwood log grading.

Table 7.4   Allowable pith deviations

Log diameter (cm)	Maximum deviation of pith from centre (mm)	
	Well centred	*Reasonably central*
30–46	25	25
46–61	32	64
61–76	39	76
76+	51	102

References

Forestry Commission (1989). *Marketing for small woodlands. County list of mills, merchants and contractors.* Forestry Commission, Edinburgh.
Thompson, D.A. (1988). Marketing chains for broadleaves. In *Broadleaves – changing horizons,* ed. M.J. Potter. Institute of Chartered Foresters, Edinburgh.

8 Improving poor quality woodland to produce timber

Poor quality woodland can be defined as an inferior crop which has a poor stocking of marketable species, other than for firewood, and where the majority of trees are of poor form or defective (poor does not imply inferior for other objectives such as amenity and wildlife conservation). However, many poor quality woodlands are on fertile sites capable of producing valuable timber. The present condition of this woodland is often due to past treatment such as war-time fellings or creaming of high quality stems which was not followed by well-managed planting or recruitment of young replacement trees, rather than an inherently poor site. There are three main characteristics of poor quality woodland: poor stocking, poor form and unmarketable species.

Poor stocking: woodland with a low stocking density does not make full use of a site's timber growing potential. Given an objective of growing quality broadleaved timber stocking must be above the following levels:

- for stands of 50–100 years: 150 utilisable stems ha^{-1};
- for stands beyond establishment but younger than 50 years: 300 utilisable stems ha^{-1}.

Poor form and other defects: i.e. where the majority of potential timber trees do not have a reasonably straight defect-free butt of at least 3 m length.

Unmarketable species: in poor quality woodland more than half the crop usually consists of species such as dogwood, elder, hazel, holly, rowan, sallow and thorns. However, the presence of many species is not itself a disadvantage unless the species are not readily marketable.

Silvicultural options

Silvicultural decisions about woodland can only be made with adequate knowledge of the structure of the woodland. The main points to observe are:

1. The number of trees which have the potential to produce quality timber.
2. The timber producing species; those that are thriving are a good guide to what to plant.
3. The spatial distribution of utilisable trees: is this patchy or uniform?

The condition of the woodland will dictate, to some extent, what options are appropriate; the flow chart (Figure 8.1) shows how the condition of a woodland can influence the choice of possible silvicultural treatment. Four main options are shown in Figure 8.1 and consideration of each forms the rest of this chapter. Of course for any one woodland more than one treatment may be appropriate or treatments may be combined.

Plate 50 A typical small neglected woodland on a farm. Appearances deceive: note fallen trees, gaps and low stocking, and no attempt at regeneration.

(38484)

Enrichment planting

This is the restocking of gaps that occur naturally or are created by group felling. Enrichment is an expensive operation and should only be considered if all of the following points can be satisfied.

1. There must be adequate levels of light to ensure early and continued growth of planted trees. Gaps should initially have a diameter of at least $1\frac{1}{2}$ times the height of the surrounding trees; frequent thinning at the edges of the group will be required to allow space for the development of the new crop. Planting should generally occur in the centre of any opening to maximise the amount of light incident on the young trees.

2. The trees must have adequate protection. Treeshelters are ideal in these situations and are widely used, however, they require considerable maintenance after planting and do not constitute a 'plant and leave' option. Also, only white or translucent shelters should be used, since some shading from surrounding trees will be present.

3. The trees must have adequate weed control; this is an essential operation and details are given in Chapter 3.

4. In older stands the two-storey structure which results has to be compatible with the long-term management objectives.

Thinning and improvement

Thinning for improvement seeks to maximise the potential of what is already present in a stand; there should be upwards of 150–300 well-formed stems that are free from defect, depending on age. If the canopy is tight and crowns suppressed, species such as ash, cherry and sweet chestnut may not respond and should not be counted; other species such as oak, beech and sycamore in the same situation are likely to respond and should be counted.

Once the initial criteria for the use of this method have been met the chosen trees should be marked in a similar way to that described on page 62, and thinning should favour the marked trees. In thicket or pre-thicket stage a utilisable crop will usually develop without the need for cleaning unless the site is subject to invasive weeds such as clematis, rhododendron, or vigorous bracken. In woodland between thicket and pole stage, trees should be inspected and tending operations carried out at least once every 4 years. Climbers should be cut or removed and all competing shrubs and trees cut to allow complete crown freedom of selected trees.

Coppicing

Almost all broadleaved species coppice vigorously. A ready market for firewood and hardwood pulp can make the operation profitable and it is a simple way of coping with poor quality woodland. However, no stand improvement is effected, the prospects for creating high forest by storing coppice stems of the best species are uncertain, and it is only feasible if timber species predominate, i.e. it is an unsuitable treatment for poor quality woodland mainly consisting of species such as elder, sallow or thorns.

Where expenditure must be severely limited and care of the stand likely to be only intermittent, working the woodland on a coppice cycle as a whole, or preferably in three or four compartments at different stages of the cycle, can be the best management choice. Input is low, some return can be expected at each coppicing, working is concentrated as much as possible, and a varied woodland structure is created which increases ecological diversity. It is well suited to small woods of mixed tree species in relatively inaccessible places This is not a system for producing quality timber.

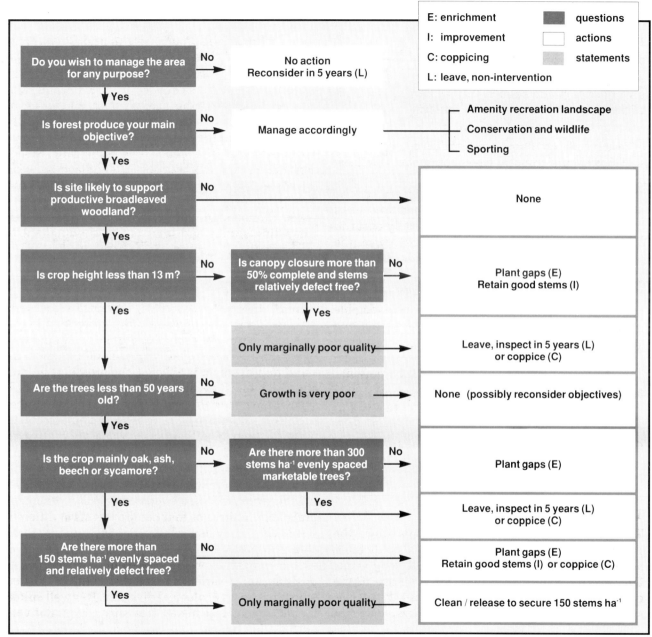

Figure 8.1 Silvicultural options for managing neglected woodland.

Plate 51 Removal of dead trees in this woodland could form a centre to start group enrichment planting or be deliberately left for conservation. (38172)

Plate 52 A small group enrichment planting: unfortunately the trees are suffering from a lack of weed control. (40208)

The 'do nothing' option

Non-intervention may sometimes be the best decision, i.e. not to manage a woodland for a period of time. *Woodland does not benefit from prolonged neglect* and a decision to leave should not be equated with abandonment. Two factors may lead to choosing this option.

- **Condition of woodland.** There is never any point in treating woodland just for the sake of it, and well-established, previously managed woods can usually survive a decade without any attention apart from squirrel control. A stand may be left provided it is not 'going back' (crown dieback, defective stems, overmaturity, browsing damage), and providing that potential crop trees are not being suppressed, and human safety is not at risk.

- **Economic reasons.** The low commercial value of poor quality woodland is often partly due to poor access. Thus, where there are no other pressing reasons or liabilities, careful timing of operations to coincide with a good market for produce to maximize revenues may mean the difference between substantial outlay and profit. A few years' delay can be rewarded in this way, but to take advantage of it an owner or agent must be constantly aware of market trends; it should not be an excuse for neglect.

Plate 53 Woodlands can often appear neglected but closer inspection frequently reveals potential for thinning and improvement. (38537)

Plate 54 Coppicing is a simple management system suitable for many broadleaved woodlands.

(37244)

Further reading

Forestry Commission Publications

Bulletins
62   Silviculture of broadleaved woodland
69   Beech bark disease
75   The silviculture and yield of wild cherry
78   Natural regeneration of broadleaves
91   The timbers of farm woodland trees
93   Ash dieback – a survey of non-woodland trees
100 Honey fungus
102 Forest fencing

Handbooks
1   Forest insects
2   Trees and weeds
6   Forestry practice
7   Treeshelters
8   Establishing farm woodlands

Field Book
8   The use of herbicides in the forest

Forest Record
124 The fallow deer

Arboricultural Leaflet
10   Individual tree protection

Arboricultural Research Note
60/88/ENT   Oak defoliation

Occasional Papers
31   Factors affecting the natural regeneration of oak in upland Britain
32   Price–size curves for broadleaves
36   The long term global demand for and supply of wood
37   UK demand for and supply of wood products

Research Information Notes
149 Selection of superior oak
153 Hopper modification for grey squirrel control
180 Grey squirrel damage control with warfarin
191 Grey squirrels and the law
198 Vegetative propagation of oak using coppice shoots
214 Occurrence of decline and dieback of oak in Great Britain
218 Shake in oak
223 Do dominant oaks have few epicormic branches?

Other Publications

MATTHEWS, J.D. (1990). *Silvicultural systems.* Clarendon Press, Oxford.

PHILLIPS, D.H. and BURDEKIN, D.A. (1992). *Diseases of forest and ornamental trees.* Revised edn. Macmillan, London.

PRIOR, R. (1983). *Trees and deer.* Batsford, London.

SAVILL, P.S. (1991). *The silviculture of trees used in British forestry.* C.A.B. International.

SAVILL, P.S. and EVANS, J. (1986). *Plantation silviculture in temperate regions.* Clarendon Press, Oxford.

Index

(Where headings are followed by a string of references the most important are printed in **bold** type. The seven species with which this Handbook is primarily concerned – ash, beech, wild cherry (gean), oak (pedunculate and sessile), sweet chestnut, and sycamore – are not separately indexed, since they occur on nearly every page. Users, therefore, requiring information about pruning sycamore, for example, should consult the heading 'pruning'.)

sweet chestnut: *see introductory note*
sycamore: *see introductory note*

tendering 78
textile equipment 15
thinning 17, 18, 30, 31, 34, 37, 41, 43, 47, 58,
    61–67, 71, 74, 86, 89
    cycle 62, 65
    intensity 62, 65
    systematic 62
    types 62–63
thorns 84, 86
tool handles 15, 18
transplants 25
    size 24–27
    see also planting stock
transport industry 7
tree guards 52; *see also* treeshelters
treeshelters 10, 22, **27, 29–30**, 46, 52, 58, 86
turnery 15, 19, 74
tussock grass 24, 34

undercuts 26
understorey planting 11, 70–71
United States 6
uses, of timber 7, 15, 74, 79

veneer quality timber 7, 15, 19, 74, 75, 76; *see also*
    quality classes
voles 28, 33, 34, 48, 51–52; *see also* mammals,
    damage by

warming, global 6
weeds 9, 38, 46, 86
    control 11, 22, 24, 29, 31, **32–34**, 37, 38, 41, 43,
        44, 47, 52, 86; *see also* herbicides
weevil, large pine 58–60
wild cherry: *see introductory note*
wildlife habitats 1, 6, 84, 87
willow 8, 23, 56; *see also* sallow
windthrow, windsnap 41, 48; *see also* storms
    (1987, 1990)
wolf trees 63, 67
woolly aphid 27, 58
working qualities, of timber 14–15

yield 65–66

This index was prepared by Dr John Chandler.

Printed in the UK for HMSO Dd 0294456 3/93 C50 3937/2B 12521